The 31st Fighter Group in World War II

BY RON MACKAY

COVER PAINTINGS BY DON GREER

COLOR ILLUSTRATIONS BY DON GREER AND DAVE GEBHARDT

Squadron/Signal Publications

Front Cover: Off the coast of Italy, a Spitfire Mk. V (Tropicalized) of the 31st Fighter Group's 308th Fighter Squadron escorts its replacement, a P-51B, as Mt. Vesuvius erupts in the distance. In March 1944, the same month the 308th saw its beloved Spitfires replaced by the Mustang, the volcano covered the surrounding area with lava cinders.

Back Cover: 31st Fighter Group commanding officer Col. Bill Daniel, in his P-51D *Tempus Fugit*, attacks a Messerschmitt Bf 109G. In addition to the usual "candy stripe" Group markings, Daniel's Mustang carries a red replacement red rudder from an airplane of another P-51 group, probably the 332nd.

If you have any photographs of aircraft, armor, soldiers or ships of any nation, particularly wartime snapshots, why not share them with us and help make Squadron/Signal's books all the more interesting and complete in the future? Any photograph sent to us will be copied and the original returned. The donor will be fully credited for any photos used. Please send them to:

Squadron/Signal Publications, Inc.
1115 Crowley Drive
Carrollton, TX 75006

Left: The official insignia of the 31st Fighter Group, approved 28 June 1941, depicts a shield divided diagonally by a wavy line into blue and gold segments. At upper right is a legless wyvern (a winged two-legged dragon with a barbed tail) with wings raised. The group's motto, "Return with Honor," appears on a gold ribbon below the shield.

Acknowledgements

My eternal thanks go to Ed Dalrymple, former "original" Spitfire pilot with the 31st Fighter Group, who was a principal guiding light for me in completing this book. I hope he enjoys the ramblings of this "bloody Highlander"! Grateful thanks also go to Elmer "Buzz" Howell. The vast amount of information made available to me via the group association's newsletters and microfilms are due to the efforts of these two fine gentlemen. Other names who come to mind are Dennis Kucera, "Ossie" Ausborn, Yancy Tarrant, Roger Zierenburg, "Andy" Anderson, Roland Root, and Bob Goebel; Bob's fine book, *Mustang Ace*, was another comprehensive source of detailed information. I must apologize for not mentioning the names of other ex-31st Fighter Group members, as there is simply not enough room to do so. To all of you — named or anonymous — I can only say, "Thanks a million!"

Title Page: P-51D *Bonnie II* of Maj. George T. Buck, who commanded the 309th Fighter Squadron from 12 October 1944 to 16 February 1945.

The 31st Fighter Group, which was to create a proud record in the Mediterranean Theater of Operations (MTO) during World War II, was created from another fine Army Air Forces unit, the 94th Fighter Squadron. The 94th had been born during World War I as the 94th Aero Squadron, one of whose famed aviators was Eddie Rickenbacker, and his example of skilled aggression in the art of aerial combat was to be upheld by the fledgling group's pilots.

The 31st Fighter Group was constituted as the 31st Pursuit Group (Interceptor) on 22 December 1939 and activated at Selfridge Field, Michigan, on 1 February 1940. Its first commanding officer was Lt. Col. Harold George, who later, after promotion to brigadier general, would command all air units in the Philippines as a member of Gen. Douglas MacArthur's staff.

Squadron numbers 39, 40, and 41 were assigned to the group, but these numbers would not be carried into action.

In the fall of 1941, the new unit took part in the Army's war games held in the southern United States. These exercises were carried out under conditions which were particularly hard, especially on the ground crews, who found themselves obligated to operate under very spartan surroundings. However, this was to prove a blessing in disguise when the Group arrived in North Africa a year later to find similar operating conditions, the men already having been toughened by their experience during the war games.

The 31st was assigned P-35s in the beginning, but these had been replaced by P-40s and then by the Bell P-39 Airacobra by the time the war games took place. Hardly had the games concluded, when the country found itself at war. Orders came for the squadrons to be sent to the West Coast but without the parent group. The 31st remained in position and in January 1942 was assigned the 307th, 308th, and 309th Fighter Squadrons with which it would go to war. It was redesignated 31st Fighter Group in May 1942.

Training of the new squadrons' pilots and ground crews at New Orleans was hurried along, because rumors about an impending assignment to a combat zone were confirmed in May. By this time, the key personnel who would lead the Group into action had all been appointed. Col. John "Shorty" Hawkins was group commanding officer, having taken over from Col. George on 1 July 1941. Lt. Col Albert Clark was executive officer. Squadron commanders were Maj. Marvin McNickle (307th Fighter Squadron), Maj. Fred Dean (308th

(Above) Three of the 31st Fighter Group's P-39s warm up for a mission during the Army's war games in North and South Carolina, November 1941. The cross applied to the fuselage denoted service in one of the two "opposing forces" involved in the games.

(Above) Early days in England. Spitfire Mk. Vbs of the 308th Fighter Squadron are lined up off the perimeter track at Atcham, the Group's first overseas base. Markings feature a yellow surround to the fuselage insignia and the placing of individual aircraft letters lower than squadron codes.

Ground crew observe the results of brake failure on this Spitfire Mk. Vb, which occurred when Sgt. Howell was taxiing it back to its Kenley dispersal on August 1942. The nickname "Buzz" stuck to Howell ever after, but Group Commanding Officer Col. Dean praised his action, which prevented more serious damage. Individual aircraft letter is higher than squadron code letters, and the national insignia has no yellow surround.

Maj. Avery of the 308th Fighter Squadron climbs out of his Spitfire Mk. Vb as his crew chief stands by for a report and other ground crew attend to the fighter. Avery became commanding officer of the squadron in September 1942.

FS), and Maj. Harrison Thyng (309th FS). The Group was to be transferred to England, but the proposed method of transfer was met with little enthusiasm by the pilots. The plan was for a mass flight of the Group's aircraft via Greenland and Iceland, relying on navigational guidance from B-17s of the 97th Bomb Group. No doubt it was with relief that the pilots heard this plan had been abandoned. This was because the 31st's new batch of P-39s, which were originally due to be picked up at the Bell factory in New York before the Group proceeded to England, were now earmarked for the West Coast as the Japanese threat, which would climax in June at the Battle of Midway, continued to develop. Movement overseas would now be by ship.

Early days in England. One 308th FS mechanic refuels HL-U, while a second polishes the canopy, and a third attends to the radio. At this stage, most of the Group's support equipment, such as the fuel truck, was supplied by the RAF.

On 4 June 1942, the same day the fortunes of war in the Pacific took a drastic turn for the better with the U.S. Navy's victory over the Japanese at Midway, the ground crew of the 31st Fighter Group stepped on board the mighty liner *Queen Elizabeth* berthed in New York harbor. Ahead of them lay five to six days of fast sailing across the North Atlantic to Britain, the ship steaming independently and relying on its high speed to outpace any intercepting U-boats. The vessel was literally packed from stem to stern with "Sad Sacks," who in many cases became even sadder due to seasickness. Sleep was never easy for those unaccustomed to having to do so in hammocks, while "Abandon Ship" and other drills took up an element of their waking time. Already the men were becoming accustomed to British naval terms such as "ack-ack" and "pom-pom guns," and announcements such as "The smoking lamp is lit." What they could not have envisaged was the degree to which they would also absorb Royal Air Force terminology in the months ahead.

Their arrival at Gourock, Scotland, on 9 June was met with surprise by one of the men (reputedly from New Jersey), who exclaimed "Scotland? I t'ought we was goin' to England!" Debarkation actually took place the following day, and, hampered by their gear, the men wearily straggled aboard the train that would deliver them to their assigned airfield at Atcham, Shropshire. On the way, the train stopped right on the Scottish-English border. An inquiring G.I. hailed a man on the platform: "Say, where are we at?" The man replied, "The front of the train is in England, the rear in Scotland." A second G.I. asked, "What's the difference?" The answer was, "The Scots are better Englishmen than the English!"

At the end of a wearying fourteen-hour rail journey, the men settled down at their new base for what would be a relatively short

eight weeks. In that time, much adaptation would take place, not only to their surroundings but also and more vitally to their future combat role and equipment. Having flown P-39s for the past year, the group's personnel expected to be reunited with Bell's powerful if eccentric fighter. Their reaction to the news that they would be flying the legendary Spitfire must have been startling. It wasn't that the P-39 was particularly deficient; what was surprising was the fact that although the Spitfire had already been successfully tested in battle, the performance of the current Mark V Spitfire was deficient

Lt. Schofield of the 307th FS practices a "scramble," watched by Lt. Sargent (right). Fighter's wing-root area is well scuffed by feet of both pilots and mechanics. Cockpit door contains a crowbar for emergency use. Schofield is wearing RAF-pattern flying boots.

(Below) His Spitfire Mk. Vb plugged in to the "trolley-ack" (short for "trolley accumulator," RAF term for the auxiliary battery cart standing on right), Lt. Wooten (307th FS) prepares to enter the cockpit at Merston, September-October 1942. Shirt-sleeve dress may indicate a nonoperational flight. The name *Lima Challenger* reputedly refers to the purchase of the aircraft with funds provided by Mr. H.L. Woodhouse of Lima, Peru. Aircraft serial (EN851) is repeated in small characters on upper fin. This Spitfire was converted to a Seafire IB in 1943 and given the new serial number NX952.

(Above) Pilots of the 31st Fighter Group mingle with their RAF contemporaries from 412 Squadron, Merston. It was while he was detached to this Canadian unit that Group Executive Officer Col. Clark went down over France to become a prisoner of war, the first of the 31st FG to suffer such a fate. Maj. Thyng (309th FS CO) is third from right. The wartime censor painted out all details on the horizon in order to conceal the location.

(Below) A 308th FS Spitfire Mk. V is rigged for gun tests on the airfield at Gibraltar just before the North African invasion on 8 November 1942. The national insignia has a yellow surround, a marking style in regular use in the Mediterranean theater until mid-1943.

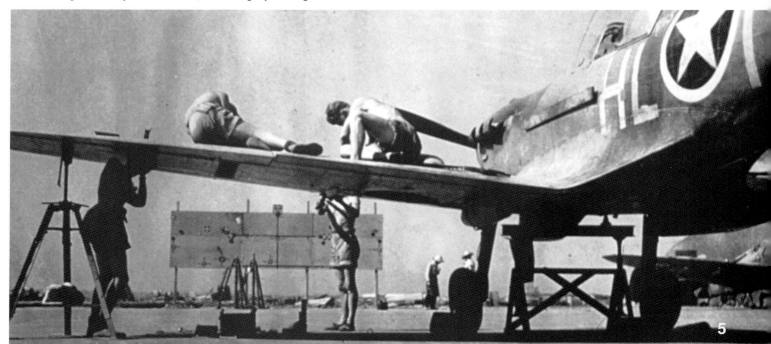

(Above) A formation of Spitfires of the 309th FS while the squadron was based at Westhampnett, England. An enterprising 309th pilot probably took the photo, although it is unlikely the squadron was flying a combat mission at the time.

(Above) Second Lt. Joe Byrd (309th FS) stands under the nose of his Spitfire Mk. V at Westhampnett, England. The lieutenant was killed 8 November 1942 when his fighter was struck by gunfire from French D.520s as he touched down at Tafaroui.

(Above) A relaxed group of pilots of "B" Flight, 308th FS, at Westhampnett on 22 September 1942. Standing on left is Capt. Frank Hill, a future squadron and Group CO, and third from left is Lt. M. P. Smith (missing in action over Pantellaria, 11 June 1943). Kneeling second right is Lt. Ed Dalrymple.

(Below) A pair of 308th FS Spitfire Mk. VBs at Atcham during the Group's training period contrasts sharply with the horse-drawn cart trundling peacefully along the perimeter track.

(Above) The Spitfire's propeller ground clearance was small, especially when running over rough surfaces, and ground clearance (or more properly, lack of it) was the probable cause for the nosing over of MX-Z of the 307th FS. Wooden propeller blades have been sheared off.

(Below) Lts. Jerry Collingsworth (left) and Woody Thomas of the 307th FS at Merston on 24 September 1942. Collingsworth went on to score six kills before completing combat duties in mid-1943. In sad contrast, Thomas was killed in action over Pichon on 8 March 1943.

Unusual code letters ("JO-JO") on tail boom of this P-38 at Westhampnett in late August 1942 do not correspond with those known to have been assigned to any P-38 unit based in England. The aircraft is probably from the 1st FG, which was stationed at nearby Ibsley between August and November, when it was transferred to North Africa.

when compared to the Luftwaffe's formidable Focke Wulf Fw 190, now entering service.

The changeover to Spitfires was to be even more a challenge for the 31st's mechanics. For example, there was little difficulty in swapping parts between individual P-39s. This was not so with the Spitfire, many of whose components such as cowlings, doors, and even skin panels were custom-fitted. In some cases it was easier to change a Spitfire's complete engine rather than try to fit a replacement part. Valuable assistance was rendered to the initially bewildered American mechanics by Royal Air Force airframe and engine mechanics, known as "fitters," who taught them the ins and outs of British aircraft maintenance. "Buzz" Howell (308th Fighter Squadron) recalls Sgt. "Bill" Goodman as one of the outstanding RAF teachers. One valuable lesson learned was the technique for adjusting the Spitfire's Merlin engine supercharger ("boost," in RAF terminology) controls to gain maximum power as well as allow emergency over-boost (pushing the throttle "through the gate"). Bill noted the Spitfire V's boost pressure settings ranged from 4 inches Hg below to 10 inches Hg above specification. Using an altimeter pressure chamber to calibrate the boost controls, he set the required limits. This practice was subsequently found to be necessary when future replacement aircraft — Spitfires and P-51s — arrived.

The whole vocabulary of RAF slang had to be quickly absorbed, particularly since the Group was expected to be combat-ready by the end of July. As it was nearly mid-summer, there was plenty of daylight available for training, but whenever possible, those off-duty could visit the local hostelries, prominent among which was the "Mitten and Mermaid." Getting to and from there on their bicycles along and usually on the wrong side of the twisting English lanes inevitably resulted in many bruised bodies, particularly on the return journey!

On 26 June the pilots arrived after a protracted voyage of twenty-five days; their scruffy merchant ship *Ranpura* was part of a convoy and was accordingly held back. The accommodations and food aboard ship matched the vessel's appearance, according to those who were unfortunate enough to take passage.

The pilots began their conversion training the next day on Miles Master advanced trainers before advancing to Mk. I Spitfires. The Spitfire was a "tail dragger," having conventional landing gear and a tail wheel, unlike the tricycle landing gear of the P-39, and

ground loops and nose-overs were common. Moreover, the Spitfire did not require the power for landing that had been demanded by the P-39, so landed slower. However, once the gentler landing technique was learned, the pilots settled down with their new charges. Sadly, the Group's first fatality occurred within only four days when Lt. Giacomini (temporary 308th FS leader until relieved by Maj. Fred Dean) died in an attempted emergency landing. Lt. Kerr (309th FS) was a second fatal training casualty on 18 July; he was making an oxygen test flight, and it was assumed he blacked out and never recovered before impact. In addition, there were at least two midair collisions during training; fortunately, neither of these resulted in loss of a pilot, although one Spitfire had a wing tip chewed off by the other's propeller. In just over two weeks, twenty-one aircraft were involved in accidents, including one in which the pilot had to be pulled out of his overturned fighter. Such an attrition rate could not be sustained if the Group was to function properly, and at an officers meeting, the pilots were forcefully reminded by Col. Hawkins to be less casual in their flying techniques and procedures.

The Spitfire had its drawbacks, among them the cockpit, which was a tight fit for even an average-sized man. The narrow landing gear was prone to collapse if the aircraft swerved on takeoff or landing, or was clumsily set down. Taxiing a Spitfire was an art, given the long engine cowling that blocked any direct forward view from the cockpit. One RAF garment quickly adopted by the pilots was a silk scarf. There was no glamour in this, only the need to prevent neck chafing as a constant all-round scrutiny was kept for hostile aircraft.

The Group's first sight of the Luftwaffe at close hand was far removed from the combat zone. Three captured enemy aircraft from a group of the same used by the RAF for orientation (and known as the "RAFWaffe") landed at Atcham. A Junkers Ju 88 and Heinkel He 111 were accompanied by a Messerschmitt Bf 109, the latter attracting special attention, in particular its magnificently engineered Daimler-Benz engine.

Gunnery training was undertaken at RAF Valley, Wales, from early July, a support party having arrived two days previously. Each pilot tested his skill with the Spitfire's two 20 mm cannon and four .303-caliber machine guns. Some results were spectacular, with one pilot recording hits (reputedly not fatal) on the target-tow aircraft. A second incident involved an RAF airman who, while

Maj. Thyng about to enter the cockpit of a Spitfire Mk. Vb still bearing RAF markings. Thyng was the 309th FS's first CO in Europe.

A Spitfire V of the 309th FS lifts off from Westhampnett. U.S. national insignia is fully applied under the wing, but the fuselage insignia appears to be incompletely painted over the original RAF roundel.

A jaunty Lt. Ed Dalrymple (308th FS) alongside his Spitfire. Dalrymple was an original Group pilot who completed his tour in mid-1943, adding three kills to the Group record in the process.

sitting in Maj. Avery's aircraft, fired the guns, with the shots just missing the tea wagon!

Already, several personnel had been detached to front-line RAF fighter fields to gain combat experience, but the Group's first combat mission involved Lt. Col. Clark (air executive officer), Maj. Dean (308th FS commanding officer) and Maj. Avery. This proved to be a devastating introduction to combat for the Group. On 26 July, while flying behind the commanding officer of 412 Squadron, RAF, operating from Merston, Clark became separated during an airfield strafing mission and was picked upon by several opponents. He evaded their immediate attentions by a loop and zoom out over the Channel. Soon, his engine started to falter, and he elected to turn back into France for a successful belly landing. He was captured and ultimately ended up as "Big S" (security officer) in Stalag Luft III at Sagan, Poland. The facts of air combat had come home in a brutal manner even before the Group had entered the fray.

The Group's first move "down south" occurred on 30 July, when advance parties started out for three airfields, the 307th FS going to Biggin Hill, 308th FS to Kenley, and the 309th FS to Westhampnett; the transfers were completed by 2 August.

"Buzz" Howell was to acquire his nickname soon after reaching Kenley. He recalls:

"I had taxied HL-L [crew chief Jim Leister] about four hundred yards from Engineering, turned off the taxiway at the revetment, and stopped to wait for a mechanic to direct me; there were two aircraft already parked there. The brakes were on, as it was slightly downhill into the revetment.

"As I waited the plane began moving forward. I checked the air-brake pressure gauge … it read zero! I did the first thing that came to mind to avoid rolling into the other two aircraft … kicked full left rudder and 'popped' the throttle. The plane turned left onto the grass okay, but the right wing struck the fence around a transformer near the revetment. The airplane turned violently back to the right and slid sideways. Both main landing gear legs folded up to the right, and the Spitfire came to a stop about fifteen feet from the Armament Shack where some fifteen to twenty men were working

Lt. Carl Payne's combat career began with several incidents, including the crash landing of his Spitfire Mk. V during Operation Torch. His fighter bears a U.S. flag along with the name *Peter* below the cockpit. The large Vokes air filter under the cowling has been crushed by the impact.

Spitfire "bone yard" at La Senia, Algeria, holds the carcasses of several aircraft. None carry full codes, and the fuselage star on right-hand aircraft is a different shape. The American flag marking was intended to indicate "friendly" aircraft to the Vichy French as well as to hopefully delude them into thinking that only American forces were involved in the North African landings.

(Above) Lt. Dalrymple (308th FS) stands with two French transport pilots prior to a ferry flight from Telergma on 23 February 1943. (Below) The French Caudron C.445 Goeland transport parked next to a C-47.

The building at Casablanca used by the 308th FS's detachment when the squadron provided air cover for the Churchill-Roosevelt conference in January 1943. The men would look back on such facilities as luxurious compared to those they would endure for the remainder of the North African campaign.

Such sorties across to the French coast, but rarely further, began to create a degree of resentment among some of the 308th FS armorers. The reason lay in the fact that even if the pilots did not operate their guns, the guns still had to be cleaned after every flight. Sgt. "Andy" Anderson (an armament chief) had his men fashion sling-shots which were hung over the gun-sights with a terse note reading, "If you don't feel like firing your guns, then use these!" However, the day was rapidly approaching when such notices were to become redundant, at least for a short period.

Maj. McNickle experienced a foretaste of action on one sortie when he got in a quick burst at a German fighter. However, he then passed out and fell 12,000 feet before recovering. He was fortunate to have so much initial height in which to regain consciousness, as lack of altitude often proved fatal to pilots in similar circumstances.

In one respect the ground crews had learned their trade as well as, if not better than, their RAF "cousins." This showed in the time taken to ready aircraft for the next sortie as well as time taken to "scramble" (RAF slang for quickly getting airborne) four fighters. The 31st FG, or the 308th FS at least, beat the RAF on both counts, their reward being free beer the next time the Anglo-American parties hit the pubs!

Two Dewoitine D.520 fighters, probably at La Senia airfield, squat at their dispersal after the French surrender. Around nine hundred examples of this nimble fighter were produced following the prototype's initial flight in 1938.

inside. I cut the ignition and got out." Buzz was later told that the fuel and throttle were off and the gear handle was up. His CO's reaction left him grateful, Maj. Dean saying; "Good work, sergeant. It seems you did everything a pilot could have done to prevent greater damage."

All three squadrons were now under the tutelage of seasoned RAF pilots, who imparted their combat experience to their untried American counterparts. Some of the advice was taken almost literally to heart. Lt. Ed Dalrymple (308th FS) recalls RAF Wing Commander Brian Kingcome briefing the Group pilots to go "balls out and at absolutely zero feet." During the crossing he was horrified to see one pilot literally plowing through the Channel spray and admitted on return to Kenley that this pilot had frightened him (a Battle of Britain ace) to death! Enthusiasm tinged with caution was stressed. On another mission to the French coast with the object of luring the Luftwaffe away from the main mission force, the Wing Commander ordered "return to base" after the ground controller had reported large concentrations of fighters approaching; he clearly felt the chances of a favorable engagement for his force were poor and disengaged accordingly.

A Loire et Olivier LeO.451, its engine cowlings and center fuselage draped with tarpaulins, probably also at La Senia. The pronounced stabilizer dihedral, twin fins, and long, glazed nose were distinctive recognition features of this French medium bomber. Identity of other aircraft is unknown.

The portly shape of a Grumman Martlet IV belonging to 893 Squadron of the Fleet Air Arm and based on HMS *Formidable*. In the background are 31st FG Spitfires. This photograph is also believed to have been taken at La Senia.

Since commencing operations the Group had experienced little contact with the Luftwaffe, one exception being Maj. Thyng (309th FS CO), who had claimed one damaged enemy aircraft on 8 August, but this was soon to change. The seaport of Dieppe on the Channel coast of France had been selected for a "reconnaissance in force" to test the German defenses and assess the prospects of a future successful invasion of the Continent. The Canadians, supported by British Commandos, were to provide the main Army units. The task of the RAF was to provide fighter cover over the landing and so prevent Luftwaffe interference with what was named Operation Jubilee.

First indications that something big was imminent came on the evening of the 18th when all leave was cancelled. At Kenley, ground crew were awakened at 0300 and ordered to the flight line on alert status. Following a briefing for the pilots, they were escorted under guard to their quarters, an action which was not relaxed until all operations were completed.

The first sorties went out around 0715, signaling the start of a hard day's combat in which an average of four missions was flown. Twelve Spitfires of the 308th FS were led into action by 1st Lt. Frank Hill. Splitting into three flights, the squadron patrolled Dieppe between 8,000 and 10,000 feet. Hill was soon informed of incoming "bogies" (unidentified aircraft) from the east. These materialized into Fw 190s, which promptly dived on Hill's flight in pairs. Hill turned the flight into his opponents to make it hard for the Luftwaffe pilots to bring their fire to bear, but one burst badly damaged the left wing tip on Lt. D. K. Smith's aircraft. Finding himself behind one Fw 190, Hill directed two full bursts of cannon and bullets into its fuselage, and the fighter vomited black smoke and rolled downward. Hill followed it down to 3,000 feet but then pulled out and away to avoid his flight becoming embroiled in the hail of flak over Dieppe.

As the squadron was about to disengage and head home, Lt. Inghram (flying HL-P) radioed he was going down, but instead of engaging a target, he was seen to bail out, with his chute only fully opening as he neared the waters of the English Channel. Two vessels were spotted heading his way as he floated down. His rescuers must have been German, as he was later reported a POW. Worse for the squadron was the loss on the second sortie of Lt. Dabney (HL-J); unlike Inghram, he was killed in action (KIA).

Meanwhile the 309th FS, led by Wing Commander "Johnny" Walker, was also heavily engaged. On its second sortie, Lt. Claude McRaven, flying as number four in his section, heard Walker call for the section to attack a lone Dornier Do 217, whose crew abandoned their stricken aircraft. Turning for home, McRaven and his partner became separated and were bounced by Fw 190s. As they banked away, his Spitfire shuddered, but this he attributed to making too tight a turn. Landing near Dover, McRaven walked away without any scrutiny of his aircraft. Returning later with the intention of flying on to his base, he was asked by the ground crew if he intended to fly the fighter. The remark puzzled him until he saw the result of the shudder: a mangled elevator and rudder inflicted by enemy gunfire! Claude's return to Merston was by truck transport.

The Group's first New Year's Day while in active service (1 January 1943) was spent at La Senia. The 309th FS ground crew constructed this detailed greeting card, which is propped up in front of a Spitfire Mk. V bearing a tropical filter. Sgt. Guzzanato stands at left.

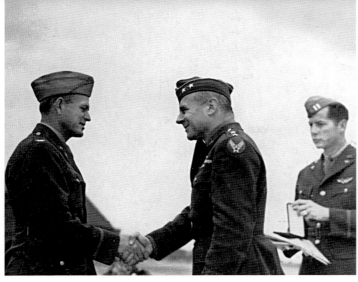

Gen. Jimmy Doolittle (center) congratulates Col. Hawkins, who has just received the Air Medal. Doolittle, who the preceding April had led a flight of Army B-25s off the aircraft carrier USS *Hornet* in the first American strike of World War II on the Japanese home islands, visited La Senia for the Group's first medal award ceremony a few days before Christmas 1942.

(Above) The unmistakable profile of a Spitfire Mk. Vb of the 308th FS, somewhere in North Africa, as indicated by the B-17 in the hangar in the background and the barren scenery. The large Vokes air filter under the nose was necessary to cope with the sandy wastes of North Africa but noticeably reduced the fighter's top speed.

The Luftwaffe did not get its way entirely. Lt. Sam Junkin (also 309th FS) was heard to holler, "I got one!" and so the Group's victory list was begun. Junkin's success was qualified, however, because almost immediately, he was forced to bail out over the Channel where he was later picked up, having been badly wounded in the shoulder. Junkin had a favorite expression to describe a tight situation: "It's rough, but it will get rougher!" As he was hauled out of the water, he saw a fellow squadron pilot standing on the deck and gasped, "Boy, it don't get no rougher!"

As he was disengaging from one combat, Maj. Thyng noticed another 31st pilot bailing out. As his parachute deployed and the pilot drifted slowly down, Thyng circled round to ensure nobody attempted to machine-gun the helpless airman. For this action in which he was ever in danger of being bounced, Thyng was awarded the Silver Star.

Due to its short landing gear, the Spitfire's propeller ground clearance at take-off was marginal, and it was all too easy to clip the runway. Sgts. Glenn Holman and Ed Leclair watched one of their 308th FS aircraft do just this on one sortie. Undaunted, the pilot continued with the mission. On return he said he had experienced some vibration, but the fighter performed otherwise normally — even though (unbeknownst to him until he had landed and shut down his engine) the propeller blades were two inches shorter!

Oversights were all too easy to make under the daylong stress of what was the Group's first major operation. The radio of one fighter on readiness alert had been replaced. Sgt. Davenport happened to look at the old set on the bench and notice the crystals still installed! The pilot was already strapped in when the crystals were taken out to the runway end where the aircraft was located and installed in record time, given that the aircraft could have been scrambled any second.

The 31st FG and its RAF comrades succeeded in deflecting the bulk of the Luftwaffe's bombing and strafing assaults from the soldiers below. This was of little avail, however, because the bulk of the troops was pinned down on the beaches, and over half the force would be dead or prisoners of wars before withdrawal. Apart from Lt. Junkin, another pilot registered a definite kill, and Lts.

(Above) Lt. Dalrymple, seen here at Gibraltar on 14 November 1942, was one of six pilots sent down the previous month to prepare large numbers of Spitfires for their participation in Operation Torch.

(Below) A Spitfire and a truck are mute witnesses to a Luftwaffe bombing assault on Thelepte airfield. Most of the destruction was borne by the units sharing the field with the 31st FG. The field was evacuated in mid-February but re-occupied a few weeks later.

(Above) The Spitfire airframe was deceptively sturdy, capable of absorbing heavy damage such as that inflicted by a heavy-caliber shell on this 308th FS aircraft. Mechanic Herb Dowling stands alongside.

Another example of the Spitfire's inherent strength is demonstrated by the hole torn around the right wing cannon mount of this aircraft. Breech covers on the two machine guns are in the raised position.

The appearance of this well-wrapped female dancer (above) at a performance in North Africa was initially greeted by howls and whistles of disappointment from the men. However, their reaction was much more positive when she shed much of her cloak to reveal a very shapely figure (below).

Robertson and Wight (307th FS), Lt. Hill, and Maj. Thyng entered "Fw damaged" claims. (Hill was a future Group commanding officer and ace.) Other claims included three kills and an Fw 190 and Do 217 damaged. However, the Group would pay a high price for this tally. Apart from the 308th's two losses, Lts. Ed Tovrea, Lewis Wells, and Bob Wight (307th FS) were downed. Wells was picked up dead out of the English Channel the next day, Tovrea was taken prisoner, and Wight was missing in action. In addition, the 309th FS's Lt. Laverne Collins was also missing.

The 31st FG had been well and truly bloodied in combat, but the pace of operations soon dropped to pre-Dieppe levels, as the Group elements were assembled together at Westhampnett (yet another famous Battle of Britain airfield) and its satellite Merston on 25 August. For the next month or so the pilots would indulge in shallow-penetration "sweeps" over the continent as well as escort bombers. During that time, Maj. Thyng would lodge the sole claim when he damaged a Ju 88 off Selsey Bill on 28 September.

The sight of numerous barrage balloons in the distance impressed some of the personnel; these were probably screening the vital naval base at Portsmouth and merchant seaport at Southampton. Equally impressive was the presence of mobile Bofors guns to defend the airfields from possible Luftwaffe hit-and-run attacks, given their proximity to the channel coastline. The airfield was attacked in this manner on 18 September when two Fw 190s shot up a Hudson. There were also night raids in the area, during which leaflets detailing the German view of the Dieppe operation were dropped.

Enlisted men of the 308 FS now moved from the relative comfort of huts at Kenley into pyramidal tents. Although there was a proper building in which to conduct their basic ablutions, washing and shaving were conducted in open-air shelters. In months to come, these facilities, though Spartan, would be reflected upon ruefully as the Group encountered the "comforts" of the North African and Sicilian terrain!

On 30 August Maj. McNickle (307th FS CO) moved up as Group Operations Officer, his post being filled by Capt. Labreche, and two days later Maj. Dean (308th FS CO) similarly moved upstairs to become air executive with Maj. Avery taking over the squadron.

A Spitfire Mk. V and (in background at left) a Mk. VIII or IX, as identified by its four-blade propeller, at Le Sers, Tunisia, on 3 May 1943. Code letters HL-L are outlined to create a "shadow-shading" effect. Only the fuselage insignia bears a yellow surround.

During early October, rumors began to abound about a further transfer, but where to was anybody's guess. Col. Hawkins (Group CO) was aware of the plans for the invasion of North Africa and therefore of the Group's involvement. Having been ordered on 1 September to send sixteen mechanics to the States, from where they would sail to Casablanca to service Spitfires, Hawkins now commented that it would have been nice at the time to have known the reason for such a move, as he then would have provided them with the proper Spitfire tool kits! This vital deficiency was promptly adjusted by the dispatch of the kits. In any event, however, no 31st FG Spitfires would go to

A trio of 309th FS officers enjoys a break on a North African beach. Lt. Kelly sits facing the camera, while Lt. Juhnke stands behind. Juhnke was killed in action over La Fouconnerie, Tunisia, on 1 April 1944. Identity of the third officer is not known.

Casablanca, and the men eventually rejoined the Group some weeks after the invasion commenced!

In fact Col. McNickle had already been called to Eighth Air Force headquarters and told to select six pilots, these to be supplemented by six RAF pilots. Their task was to make combat-ready the eighty fighters reputedly allotted the Group at Gibraltar. The party sailed to "the Rock," and on arrival McNickle called on the Station commanding officer, Group Captain Bolton. McNickle was told that he was now in charge of Gibraltar's air defenses, as his pilots would have the only operational fighters on hand! Working outdoors, often in a soaking rain, the personnel, assisted by RAF staff, more than carried out their duty, readying 360 fighters. The majority of these went either to the RAF or the 52nd FG as replacements; the 31st ended up with only thirty-six Spitfires prior to the invasion!

One of the enlisted men was Staff Sgt. Loren Keefer. He was originally selected for radar training but received on-the-job instructions in radio equipment instead. He had answered the request for volunteers from Group headquarters, and after a test involving retuning three detuned radios, he was later informed that he had been selected for Advance Party duties at Gibraltar. An overnight flight via London and Cornwell in a C-47 ended on "the Rock." Although the entire party could have been loaded on one transport, it was flown down on two. The reason for this was later explained as "at least some of you might get through!"

One day Keefer was driving a Jeep, which he had brought to a halt at the runway end to permit an oncoming B-24 to land. Suddenly the bomber's engines opened up as the pilots initiated an overshoot procedure. Then, to Loren's shocked surprise, the aircraft staggered and pitched downward to smash into the sea. Among the few on board who survived was the Canadian ace George "Screwball" Beurling, who had finished a combat tour on the besieged island of Malta.

Back in England, flying was gradually curtailed toward the middle of October. By then the Group had suffered two more fatalities, neither in combat. Capt. Chambers was lost on 1 October, and eight days later Lt. Ward (308th FS) crashed while getting in some flying time. The Spitfires were then handed over to a group of Polish pilots who agreed with the wish of some crew chiefs for a real "buzz job" ("beat-up," in RAF slang). Taking off and

(Above) A nosed-over Spitfire Mk. V displays a crumpled right wing trailing edge. The intact propeller blade suggests the propeller was stationary at the moment of impact. Light-colored uniforms confirm this incident happened after the Group's arrival in North Africa — in this case at Korba, Tunisia.

Air Marshal Sir Arthur "Mary" Coningham (right) leans on the cannon barrel of a 31st FG Spitfire. Coningham, a World War I ace, became chief of the North West African Tactical Air Force (NWATAF) in February 1943. The nickname "Mary" was a corruption of "Maori," the name for the indigenous peoples of New Zealand, Coningham's native country. Coningham later directed tactical air operations during the invasion of northwest Europe.

(Above) Lt. Dalrymple, seated in his aircraft at Le Sers, Tunisia, on 8 May 1943, demonstrates how tight a fit a Spitfire's cockpit was for any pilot, even one of slim build.

(Below) Lt. Henry Roche was one of four Minnesotans who joined the Group from the same training class in early 1943. His Spitfire's name, *Flying Cock Roche*, is a play on his surname.

disappearing out of sight, the pilots seemingly had forgotten their earlier promise. However, this was not so; skimming in over the operations hut and into a zoom, the Poles confirmed their "mad" image, turning their Spitfires into aluminum needles that stitched a frenetic pattern virtually within the airfield circuit. Those who stood on a vantage point such as an aircraft wing soon removed themselves, so close did the Polish pilots "cut the grass."

While transporting gear to Chichester railroad station on 10 October, four men of the 308th FS were seriously injured when their truck was sideswiped; all were hospitalized and subsequently transferred to a Replacement Control Depot. Among the new equipment issued were the first jeeps, whose maneuverability and toughness would prove invaluable. These arrived on the 13th, the same day the 31st FG was temporarily declared nonoperational.

Three separate parties of ground personnel were formed and directed to seaports. The 308th FS sent Party P4, headed by Capt. Riha, back north to Gourock, where the Group had debarked in June. Here the men were taken by lighter to the British transport *Orbita*, but it was the 26th before the full convoy was deemed assembled and ready to sail. A few days prior to departure, Party P38 also arrived at Gourock and boarded the U.S. transport *Argentina*. Finally, Party P14 boarded the British transport *Moulten* in Avonmouth from where the vessel sailed for Gourock on the 23rd to link up with the main convoy.

The experience of the Party assigned to *Argentina* was noticeably better compared to the other two. In particular, the food was well up to expected American standards, while the vessel's general condition was sound. In comparison, *Orbita* stank to high heaven, and the food aboard was very poor. Washing had to be done with cold salt water, and the general sanitation level was as poor as the food! Some of the British crew remarked that the high incidence of seasickness was due to "these weak American stomachs," to which one sergeant retorted, "Weak! We're heaving it just as far as any of you can!" The enlisted men's quarters were in the forecastle, where the vessel's motion through the rough Bay of Biscay was most magnified, making sleep in the hammocks very difficult. The sergeants were in better quarters aft, while the officers occupied cabins on

Several Group "volunteers" dig foxholes in the scrub-strewn plain that formed Thelepte airfield. The wearing of steel helmets by a couple of the men is a good indication of the proximity of the airfield to the front line and the Afrika Korps.

"B" deck. Conditions on *Moulten* were marginally better than on *Orbita*, but only just.

For six full days the convoy heading for what was coded Operation Torch butted its way through potentially U-boat infested waters. The Torch planners' concern was that a wolf pack intercepting the vulnerable transport convoy would cut a devastating swath through their ranks and thereby destroy any likelihood of the operation being launched, let alone succeeding. The U-boats' concentration on a small tanker convoy off the African coast about this time may have been a Godsend to the invasion force if not to the hapless tanker crews. In fact, only one transport was torpedoed, and her whole complement was transferred before she went down.

The Group's pilots had traveled on H.M.S. *Leinster* along with those of the 52nd FG and the RAF pilots, an arrangement which could have stalled the air operations for Torch had the vessel been sunk and the personnel lost! However, fortune smiled on the Allies, and *Leinster* docked safely at Gibraltar on the morning of 6 November. The next day, Gen. Jimmy Doolittle visited the fliers and gave them a briefing on the impending action and the reasons for its implementation with respect to both global strategy and the combined war effort.

Gibraltar was still shrouded in darkness when the pilots were rousted out of their beds at 0300 on 8 November. Two hours later, after a quick breakfast and preflighting of their aircraft, they were placed on alert — and there they waited. By the early afternoon, their enthusiasm had somewhat faded, just when Gen. Doolittle initiated action. He asked Col. Allison (52nd FG CO) how soon his unit could take to lift off for Oran. The answer, "A day and a half," was explained by the fact that his aircraft were parked behind the 31st's fighters. Col. Hawkins answer to the same question was "About twenty minutes."

Doolittle instructed Hawkins to land at Tafaroui rather than nearby La Senia, as the latter was deemed out of service from bomb craters. The previous day's briefing had indicated that airfield control radio, fighter control units, and signal air warning facilities would by now be in place along with a command ship; at least that was the theory, and in most respects it was to remain theory.

The 308th FS and 309th FS soon formed up and headed east. The haze and thunderstorms cleared as Oran was approached. Col. Hawkins now called up the airfield control tower then attempted to contact fighter control, and finally called the command ship, all in vain. He must have reflected on Col. Dean's (air exec) words at the briefing; "Hell, that stuff is what the generals are interested in; what we want to know is what buttons to press and what direction the enemy is."

Requesting the others to hold the airfield pattern, Hawkins, having scanned the area and noting bomb craters on the runway, aimed for a stretch of ground clear of obstructions and touched down without incident. The remaining 308th FS pilots now came down in pairs. As they were landing, however, they were harassed by unexpected French artillery fire directed from the airfield's north side. These positions were attacked and silenced by the aircraft still airborne.

The 309th FS now made its approach, believing the top cover of four aircraft overhead were the promised Hurricanes. In fact they were French Dewoitine D.520s, which now attacked the vulnerable Americans. Lt. Claude McRaven as number three was leading Lt. Byrd in on final approach, when Byrd's aircraft was hammered into a flaming mass from which nobody could subsequently rescue him. Maj. Thyng was still airborne with his section, and realizing what was happening, engaged the French aircraft. He, along with Lts. Payne and Kenworthy, culled one each out of the group, leaving the chastened survivor to reflect upon his good fortune.

The 31st had arrived as planned, but only the bulk of the air echelon — the ground support units were still on their landing beach. The absence of U.S. fuel and ammunition was serious, although a crashed C-47's tanks were to provide some of the former, and some fuel was also siphoned from wrecked French aircraft. Moving the fuel from the C-47s to the Spitfires in the dark was difficult, and it was early next morning before the fighters were fuelled and otherwise regarded as serviced.

Having slept fitfully on straw bales and rather hungry (a half can of C-rations and half a chocolate bar was their only previous meal), the pilots briefed for the dawn patrol now took to the sky, but failed in the still gloomy light to intercept a lone French bomber which dropped its load squarely on a C-47. The command ship was contacted via the radio located in the ground force commander's

Many of the facilities at Thelepte were underground. "The Captain" poses at this dug-out entrance while wearing a steel helmet in place of his service cap, which is lying on top; a 308th FS Spitfire is parked in the background.

Winston Churchill's Avro York personal transport at Grombalia, in North Africa, 2 June 1943. The aircraft carried King George VI of Great Britain on a visit to the Mediterranean Theater of Operations. The York was developed from the mighty Lancaster bomber.

tank, and a communications net was established which entailed one pilot sitting in his cockpit with his radio on and the patrolling aircraft acting as a relay to the command ship.

While the pilots had been landing at Gibraltar, the ground support personnel's convoy was sailing into the Western Mediterranean. During the night of 7-8 November, the ships changed course and headed into their allocated beachheads. Around 0400 on the 8th, both *Orbita* and *Moulten* hove to outside Arzew harbor east of Oran, and the men began clambering into landing craft to be ferried onto White Beach towards mid-afternoon. The beachhead was already secured, although heavy artillery fire was harassing the landing zone. Disgorging their human loads into the surf, the landing craft retired while the Group personnel were directed by a beachmaster to take up positions in foxholes dug by the original assault force.

The pace of unloading was badly hampered by the sloping beach, which prevented landing craft getting close enough without having to be first winched in and then towed clear. It became clear that the original intention to have the Group personnel in place at Tafaroui that day, together with the necessary ordnance and maintenance to service their aircraft, was unlikely to be achieved.

In fact it was 2200 when the by now cold, wet, and hungry GIs were roused and told to pack up. Loaded onto trucks, they set out

With its tail perched precariously on an oil drum, a propeller-less 308th FS Spitfire Mk. IX undergoes a detailed engine overhaul somewhere in North Africa. The primitive servicing conditions depicted here remained so until the Group reached a more established airfield, such as that at San Severo.

for Tafaroui, after being told that they must be ready to disperse should the convoy be ambushed (The grim news that the passage there had not yet been cleared was not divulged.). Nine half-tracks equipped with machine guns escorted the trucks, and these, boosted by a few tommy guns spread among the truckloads, was the only available defensive weaponry the convoy had. It was a nervous three-hour journey to Tafaroui, but it happily passed without incident, and spirits rose with the sight of the Group's fliers. There was still a lack of ammunition, but Lt. Elliot (308th FS engineering officer) devised a method of arming the Spitfires' guns using the French ordnance on hand. This was a timely development, inasmuch as a French Foreign Legion force of tanks, artillery, and trucks was reported rapidly approaching from their headquarters at Sidi-Bel-Abbes.

Maj. Hill (308th FS) and Capt. La Brech (307th FS) departed Gibraltar early on 9 November with the balance of the Group's aircraft. Heavy rain accompanied the pilots right up to the African coast, but they touched down in order and parked. No sooner was this action completed than shells began to strike the field from the southeast in an advancing pattern. Six pilots immediately jumped into their cockpits and took off to track down the source. Lt. Ramer strafed three trucks, and two other pilots mistakenly attacked several U.S. tanks, before the 75 mm guns causing the problem were located along with the French Foreign Legion column.

At 0640 Col. Dean and two others made the first attack on the column, their cannon shells easily penetrating the tank sides and their machine-gun bullets proving equally effective in igniting the tanks' externally mounted fuel containers; several tanks and trucks were destroyed. On one of his passes, Maj. Hill (308th FS) concentrated so hard on his target that he scraped the lower fuselage of his Spitfire against a telegraph pole. A fellow pilot scanned the aircraft for signs of oil or coolant loss but saw none, whereupon Hill resumed his strafing run. On landing, Lt. Corrigan, apparently concentrating on avoiding potholes in the runway, collided with Col. Dean's aircraft and bisected its fuselage a mere foot so behind the cockpit, but both fighters were later salvaged. Subsequent sorties by both squadrons ended with the French column being largely routed, although it took tanks of the ground force to finally halt the advance of those few Legionnaires who got as far as the airfield boundary.

Indifferent communications between the Group and the command almost resulted in tragedy when the Group was requested to silence enemy guns close to the Arzew beachhead. The leader of the attacking flight was told these were located west of the river, when in fact they were on the other side. During the ensuing series of attacks on the misidentified target, return fire fatally crippled the two aircraft dispatched on this mission. Fortunately, both pilots crash-landed safely, with one returning to Tafaroui within hours. Immediately assigned to fly a second mission, this pilot, along with his wingman, was again shot down. This time he elected to destroy his Spitfire, as he was very close to the Vichy French position which had brought him down! All three pilots regained American lines by the following morning.

Although only one pilot was killed, seven aircraft were downed, with the other six pilots returning. One arrived on the back of an Arab's donkey, having displayed the official card that stated in Arabic that anyone giving help would be rewarded. On assuring Col. Hawkins he would guard the crash-landed aircraft until it was recovered, the Arab received an extra gold piece.

During the day a convoy of fuel and ammunition had arrived, but there was still a severe shortage of food and water, which was not corrected until 10-11 November; even then it was an additional three or four days before sufficient water was on hand for other than basic uses. A similar period was to elapse before adequate bedding and clothing supplies were at hand. Group personnel had to use their ingenuity to overcome a lack of equipment. Requested to deliver a message to Division Command headquarters and having no custom-built bags, Col. Hawkins utilized a torn-off pajama leg, filled it with sand, and tied off the ends. The message was inserted in this makeshift message bag, and its delivery was duly made.

As the 10th dawned, the tired personnel braced themselves for further hard combat. In fact, the main enemy onslaught had exhausted itself, and the day was passed in flying reconnaissance sorties mixed in with several strafing runs. A state of alert still had to be maintained, as there was no certain indication that resistance to the invasion had been quashed.

The next day (11 November) was Armistice Day, and it seemed appropriate that the Vichy French Authorities would pick this date to sign their armistice with the allied forces. As far as the 31st FG was concerned, the armistice meant that the men could now find proper living quarters. This was easier for the officers; the five hundred POWs captured on the 8th had been moved out to Arzew the previous day, and their vacated accommodations were taken over.

The Group's tenure at Tafaroui lasted a mere two more days, after which a move was ordered to La Senia, where the Group would remain for almost three months, except for a detachment of elements of the 308th FS to Casablanca in January. A bad feature of the new airfield and surrounding area was the presence of many sinkholes, caused by mineral deposits in the soil being dissolved by the water that appeared in the wake of rainfalls, and which the engineers tried vainly to fill. The toilets were nauseatingly primitive, being mere holes in the concrete with footprints for accurate positioning and with no paper holders. Slit-trench toilets were dug, but these were only marginally better. The living quarters in three-story barracks were filthy, with much personal equipment and belongings (including money) still strewn around, and bedbugs were a problem until they could be blow-torched. One bright spot was the creation of a Group Consolidated Mess. The Mess Officer, Lt. Pinckney, invented a fuel-fired vat for hot water with which to clean mess kits; it was lit by a long-handled torch and became a standard piece of equipment, being known by the lieutenant's name. Numerous Group ground crews later adopted the design to heat their shacks and tents, so adding a measure of comfort.

The Group's pilots did little operational flying for the rest of November, partly due to the autumn rain rendering the airfield nearly inoperable. There was the occasional air raid alarm, but no attacks materialized. Among many of the men was the feeling they had been stuck in a back-water zone, as well as doubts as to whether it had been necessary to take over the region, such was the lack of activity. However, the possible threat of a German counterthrust could never

(Above) Maj. Frank Hill in the cockpit of his Spitfire. Hill served as CO of the 308th FS and 309th FS before assuming Group command between July and September 1943. He also ran up a confirmed score of seven Axis aircraft.

(Left) A P-38F belonging to the 27th FS of the 1st FG. After flying a number of sorties from England without meeting Luftwaffe opposition, the 1st FG was ordered to North Africa under Twelfth Air Force command, and by November 1942, its P-38s were escorting B-17 bombers against Axis targets.

With its propeller and engine cowling detached, this Spitfire (probably a Mk. V) of the 309th FS is mounted on a low-loader transport.

This damaged Spitfire Mk. V of the 308th FS has been stripped of its wings prior to being loaded up. The radio hatch on the fuselage is open. The aircraft carries double identification letters.

be discounted, even if Erwin Rommel was currently heavily engaged in fending off the advance of the British 8th Army from the eastern end of North Africa.

On 6 December, Col. Hawkins relinquished command of the 31st FG when he was transferred to XII Fighter Command. At a farewell parade, the enlisted men stood in review as Spitfires of the 308th and 309th gave an air show which included a buzz of the airfield. Lt. Col. Fred Dean now assumed the mantle of command. He knew he was following a hard act, as "Shorty" Hawkins had been well regarded by all during his years at the Group helm.

Fifteen new pilots, all from Class 42G/H, joined the Group on 15 December and were equally split between the squadrons. One of these, 2nd Lt. Virgil Fields, would become 307th FS CO before being killed in action at Anzio, and four others from the group would share the same fate.

Bad weather continued to restrict flying. One pilot returned from a patrol over the area of a torpedoed oil tanker and told the crew chief, "The prop seal is leaking," pointing to his liberally oil-smeared windshield. The crew chief replied, "Sir, the Spitfire has an electric propeller; there is no prop seal!" The pilot had presumably skimmed over the tanker, whose cargo had probably been tossed around by the sea spray, so accounting for the oil residue on the Spitfire.

On 19 December, Gen. Doolittle arrived to present medals and citations. Then it was full speed ahead for Christmas. On Christmas Eve, the 308th's Armament Section held a party during which one man ran outside and fired a complete ammunition clip from his .45-caliber pistol. The officer of the day called an immediate bunk inspection and passed down the line sniffing the muzzle of each man's weapon. When Sgt. Sreiner asked the whereabouts of one individual's weapon, he was told the gun was buried in the man's footlocker from where it had never at any time been taken out. When the officer of the day repeated the question, the frustrated enlisted man pointed to his groin, saying, "Here's my gun, sir, sniff this!" The now volatile OD was gradually calmed down, but more importantly, was persuaded that the original offender belonged to another section.

The year ended with La Senia still largely nonoperational thanks to poor weather conditions. During 1942 the Group had been bloodied in two operational theaters while functioning within two Air Forces (Eighth and Twelfth). Hard times lay ahead in 1943, but all Group personnel were ready to take on their assigned task, however difficult and protracted it might turn out to be.

January 1943 opened on a quiet note for the Allies in northwest Africa. The month saw the 31st FG still literally bogged down at La Senia, flying activity being restricted to a few patrols. This state of affairs changed on the 8th, however, when the 308th FS air echelon was alerted and instructed to await orders for departure. Two days later, twelve Spitfires took off, not eastward toward the enemy, but on a diametrically opposite course. Their destination was the Moroccan city of Casablanca. It was here that the Anglo-American conference was due to take place with U.S. President Franklin D. Roosevelt and British Prime Minister Winston Churchill the main participants, and the 31st FG had been assigned the duty of air cover. The ground echelon arrived in C-47s on 11 January, and its officers were billeted at a hotel near Cazes airfield, at which the remaining personnel were billeted in the more Spartan facilities of a hangar. It would be the end of January before the Casablanca detachment returned to La Senia, and what flying they did until then was not well coordinated. The greatest enemy was not the Luftwaffe but boredom.

Back at La Senia, the single flying incident of note for the month occurred on 20 January, when an air raid alert was sounded at 2100. Maj. Thyng (309th FS) and Capt. Mitchell (350th FG) were scrambled, but their intersecting take-off runs ended in a dramatic collision in the middle of the airfield. Miraculously, neither pilot was even injured, although both fighters caught fire and were destroyed. Maj. Thyng immediately selected a replacement Spitfire and took off, this time without incident. The resultant search for the lone Luftwaffe aircraft that had been called in ended without result.

The welcome return of the Casablanca detachment on the 29th had been preceded the day before by the movement of the 307th's ground echelon toward the front line in Tunisia, signaling impending combat action for the Group. Over the next week the squadron air echelons were dispatched to Thelepte airfield, and the ground echelons were transported by C-47 to Maison Blanche and Youks-les-Bains, from where the men were then carted by truck to Thelepte. It would be around 15 February before the majority of the Group was reunited at Thelepte, but the time spent there the first time around would be measured in days thanks to the Afrika Korps!

This Spitfire Mk. V, seen here on 2 July 1943 on Gonzo Island, was the aircraft of Group Commanding Officer Col. Fred M. Dean and bears his initials for code letters. Dean led the Group between December 1942, when he succeeded Col. "Shorty" Hawkins, and his return to the United States in July 1943.

(Above) Wrapped in a large blanket, Lt. Rich of the 308th FS flashes a "victory" sign from the gunner's position of the British Air Sea Rescue (ASR) Walrus seaplane that rescued him after he ditched off the island of Pantellaria on 11 June 1943. (Below) Lt. Mosby, also of the 308th FS, stands in the cockpit of the Walrus after Lt. Rich's recovery. The Walrus was powered by a large Bristol Pegasus engine and pusher propeller.

There were two airfields at Thelepte, the 31st FG occupying Number 1, and a P-39 group occupying Airfield Number 2 three miles distant. The term "airfield" was barely justifiable, as both locations were barren plains with no proper hangars or other buildings. Fierce winds made servicing duties, particularly refueling, extremely unpleasant. An absence of proper fuel trucks meant that aircraft had to be refueled from five-gallon cans, the personnel having to contend with being saturated by a wind-driven spray of fuel. The immediate remedy was the transfer of fuel to trailer-mounted barrels to which were attached hand pumps; this was less discomforting but still time-consuming. A positive spin-off was the supply of empty five-gallon cans; some of these were filled with sand and used for building windbreaks for the sorely tried ground crew. Other empties were used as stop-gap heaters, but the lengthy round trip along barely identifiable roads to the main fuel supply depot at Tebessa meant there was barely enough fuel to spare for this secondary but equally important use.

Living and sleeping conditions at Thelepte were primeval. Only two-man pup tents were on hand at the start, and apart from freezing, the men also found it impossible to keep sand from entering everywhere. Some enterprising souls made their own Sibley tent stoves and stovepipes from salvaged mess-hall cans. Salvaged metal tubing was inserted in the stoves with which to channel the 100-octane fuel from the external supply can. Valves formed from fuel hoses and restricted by "C" clamps were a further refinement to control fuel-flow. Toilet facilities were equally basic; helmets were used for washing and shaving and canteen water used for brushing teeth. Unbeknown to the men was the fact that this type of existence would generally be their lot right through the North African and Sicilian Campaigns and right up to Pomigliano, Italy, in November!

A mission on 10 February proved to be a virtual disaster. Twelve Spitfires from the 308th escorted P-39s to Kairouan. An incorrect homing vector, coupled with very poor visibility, resulted in ten aircraft overshooting to the southwest and force landing. Maj. Avery (308th FS CO) suffered badly cut hands, Lt. Smith received head lacerations, and Lt. Corrigan injured his back in the landings. Two aircraft were wrecked, but the others were serviced the next day by a detachment and flown back to Thelepte; the wrecks were transported back for use as spare parts. Capt. Hill now took temporary squadron command.

El Aouina airfield near Tunis was littered with abandoned Axis aircraft, including this duo of Macchi C.200 fighters, seen here 18 June 1943. Note distinctive engine cowling with bulged covers for cylinder heads and the open cockpit. The aircraft's general flying performance approached that of the Spitfire Mk. V.

The battlefront was only some forty miles west, and the Allied airfields were under imminent threat of surprise attack. On the 15th, four Bf 109s, escorted by a similar number of Fw 190s, stormed in over Thelepte at low level. A 308th FS flight patrolling the base engaged the intruders, with Lt. Callander destroying one Bf 109 and Lt. D. K. Smith damaging a second. Their success was blunted by the loss of Lt. Reed, whose aircraft burst into flames and headed straight for a British gun position. Lt. Reed gallantly succeeded in pulling his doomed fighter up and over the site, but immediately afterward the aircraft nosed in and Reed was killed. A subsequent recommendation for a medal for Reed to mark his sacrificial action was not approved.

On 15 February a patrol was dispatched, but the flight of four aircraft was soon reduced to three when a pilot aborted. Lt. Collingsworth (307th FS), flying as number three, sighted bogies behind and above to the right and called them in, shouting "break right" when they had closed up. The flight leader's gentle turn would have exposed Collingsworth to serious danger had he held position, so he elected to turn inside the other pair. He immediately found himself head-on with the lead Fw 190. Both aircraft fired, but

Also seen at El Aouina was this Focke Wulf Fw 190, an oil drum substituting for its smashed tail-wheel. Absence of cockpit canopy reveals the extreme length of the canopy frame, which stretched as far back as the fuselage balkenkreuz insignia. Code letters are those applied at the Focke Wulf plant, which indicates the fighter had not yet been allocated to a front-line unit by the time the Luftwaffe abandoned the airfield.

the German pilot came off worse and was forced into a hasty crash landing. Collingsworth's exited "I've got him! I've got him!" earned him an instant rebuke and a demand to maintain radio silence, but in fact Collingsworth's "kill" was a milestone as it was the squadron's first victory in aerial combat.

The U.S. Army's first full-scale effort in engaging Rommel's forces at the Kasserine Pass was an initial failure, and by 16 February the Afrika Korps was advancing ominously toward the Thelepte region. Very early on the 17th, Group personnel were awakened and ordered to pack up and stand by for evacuation. The sight of gun flashes both to the north and south was not very reassuring, holding as it did the threat of encirclement. By 0500, as loading of the available trucks was being completed, shells were impacting on the far side of the field. The 308th FS had managed earlier to commandeer ten extra trucks from Tebessa and were able to evacuate a good portion of their materiel; the other two squadrons were not so fortunate and were forced to abandon most of their gear to the enemy.

Capt. Hill's account of the evacuation is detailed:

"During the evening of the 16th, Col. Dean briefed all squadron COs on the deteriorating ground situation and mentioned the possibility of evacuation, while simultaneously assuring all that a minimum of forty-eight hours' notice would be given. This was despite the stream of trucks heading either northwest toward Tebessa or northeast into the battle zone and the ever-increasing volume of gunfire. I packed my gear, just in case!

"At 2 A.M. I was awakened by Lt. O'Brien [Operations], who had stumbled through the dark to my dugout to say Fred [Col. Dean] was on the telephone. He said the ground situation was getting worse and a dawn departure would now have to be effected; trucks were already on their way from Youks-les-Bains. Finding the key personnel was difficult, while scrambling around in the pitch dark proved far from easy, but Lt. Elliott [Engineering] and another operations officer were rousted out and achieved this primary aim in record time. Personally, I stowed most of my gear in a Musette bag that fitted into my Spitfire's cockpit. One basic item incapable of immediate stowage until the first mission at 0900 was made were the ground starter units.

"The first two trucks arrived at 0400 and were loaded with the squadron records. Four more arrived as dawn broke and we loaded them in even quicker time, spurred on by the artillery fire just over a ridge of southern-facing low hills. It was at this point we heard the 307th FS had been forced to abandon much of their equipment as well as being told that no more trucks would be coming. As a result, all but the most vital equipment had to be unloaded, and those men without transport were directed to set out on foot for Tebessa, carrying what gear they could.

"Huge fires could be seen springing up as all equipment of possible value to the Germans was destroyed. We were still sorting our gear when — miracle of miracles — across the field came no less than twelve trucks, which were promptly split between the three squadrons. Most packing was accomplished by the time the pilots were called to make their mission, which was an escort to P-39s attacking Sbeitla. The mission was routine, and we landed at Tebessa after forging our way there in the face of poor weather conditions. On landing we found the squadron cooks had salvaged the pancake batter and were dishing out hot cakes along with coffee — a real morale booster after the depressing event earlier in the day.

A Spitfire Mk. IX of the 309th FS. The practice of applying double letters to identify each aircraft appears to have been a regular practice only of this squadron.

"The main lesson to be learned from this action was the need for communications, whether by radio or using runners; everyone can respond if they know what the position is and what has to be done. In a mere seven hours we had the entire Group packed and on the way with the aircraft airborne on their mission. As the last Spitfires took off, shells were landing in the ravine area where, mere hours before, tents and mess halls were located."

The Group's fighters — apart from those of the 308th, who decamped to La Kouif two days later — remained at Tebessa for just four days. Then all three squadrons linked up once again at Youks-les-Bains to be joined by the ground support teams at yet another location — Kalaa Djerda — around the 24th. A Ju 88 unfortunate enough to cross the path of the 308th as the squadron moved to Youks on the 22nd was summarily dispatched. (When La Kouif also came under threat of enemy occupation, the 308th FS servicing teams that had joined their aircraft there were temporarily sent to an RAF base at Canrobert before later being allowed to return to Kalaa Djerda.) The Group would not be reassembled as a complete unit until the middle of April.

Air action in this short but hectic mid-February period was steady. The 308th flew three missions on the 22nd; on the last of these, Capt. Hill's flight sighted and followed a Junkers Ju-87 back to its field, where Hill downed it. The next day the squadron engaged a flight of Bf 109s but could only claim three probables and one damaged.

Kalaa-Djerda was an improvement on Thelepte. Although the large house taken over in the local town was somewhat run-down, it at least had lighting and running water. By now the German advance had been halted and was facing a counteroffensive that soon drove its forces back to their start-lines. Weather conditions for flying were variable, and little contact was made with the Luftwaffe, although Capt. G. Johnson (308th FS) did claim one damaged Fw 190 on 3 March. It must have been with mixed feelings that a move back to Thelepte was initially commenced on the 9th; this was completed a few days later. All dugouts had to be reconstructed after the Germans had destroyed them.

The day prior to the move back to Thelepte, Lt. Collingsworth (307th FS) was second element leader to Lt. Mitchell with Lt. "Woody" Thomas flying Collingsworth's wing. The low ceiling of 1,000 feet forced the flight to hold at around 600 feet, where it made an easy target for ground fire. Sighting tracers, Mitchell turned sharp left, but Collingsworth delayed his element's turn to avoid the fire before following. At this point, Thomas, who had

inadvertently pulled in front of Collingsworth during the turn, was now in the number-three position before falling back into his allotted slot. Hearing gunfire, Collingsworth was shocked on glancing back to see his wingman's aircraft inverted and in flames before it plunged into the ground and exploded.

The Fw 190 responsible was attempting to slow down to get on Collingsworth's tail, but he managed to pull up into the cloud. Emerging after a few seconds, he saw three aircraft in a Lufbery circle with a single Fw 190 off to one side. The '190 pulled full power upon seeing the Spitfire, whereupon Collingsworth, who had a slight altitude advantage, selected emergency boost in order to keep up. The Fw 190 pilot then went into a tight left turn, unaware that Collingsworth by now had only one operable 20 mm cannon, which rendered a strike highly unlikely. The combat was resolved by the German, who apparently lost control, flipped over on his back, and plowed into the ground to burst apart.

By now uncertain of the exact compass course home, Collingsworth headed in a general westerly direction. Ten minutes into his return flight, he spotted a bogey at his 10 o'clock, which materialized into a Bf 109. As he came in behind the Bf 109, a vital piece of advice handed to him by an RAF pilot back in England came to mind and probably saved his life: "Where there is one fighter, there is quite often a second!" Sure enough, as Collingsworth split into a 180-degree turn, a second Bf 109

Two Bf 109Gs of JG 53 "Pik As" (Ace of Spades) lie abandoned on Comiso airfield in Sicily on 18 July 1943. The horizontal bars on rear fuselages indicate the aircraft belonged to II Gruppe; the fighter at left bears the markings of the Gruppen Kommandeur ahead of the balkenkreuz.

(Left) Lt. Swiger of the 309th FS was involved in another collision with a group Spitfire. He was extremely lucky to survive the resultant flip-over of his own fighter, which subsequently caught fire. (Right) The aft fuselage of the Spitfire with which Swiger collided was completely obliterated.

passed directly overhead! Regarding discretion as the better part of valor, Collingsworth broke off the combat and resumed his homeward course.

On the 12th, Lts. Mosby and Brunasky (308th FS) were just lifting off when a quartet of Bf 109s, escorted by Fw 190s, hit the field. Several of the 307th's aircraft were destroyed in return for a single "damaged" claim by Mosby. Early in the afternoon, a second attack by the Luftwaffe added to the 307th's woes but cost the attackers at least one fighter. Lt. Davis closed on the formation, and when it banked right over Thelepte's Airfield No. 2, he was in perfect position to knock down the rearmost aircraft. Delayed-action bombs dropped by the attackers made for much discomfort among the airfield personnel, but injuries were confined to one man, Sgt. Mandeville. Sadly, his stomach wound was so serious that, although he was shipped to Tebessa for full hospital treatment, he died the next day, becoming the 31st FG's first enlisted casualty. Lt. Davis added to his total next day during a protracted assault on Thelepte by taking out one Bf 109 while the airfield antiaircraft guns claimed a second. The Spitfire of Capt. Fleming (308th FS) took a severe 20 mm strike around the fuselage insignia on one mission, but the dual armor plate held up well despite being dented.

Three 309th FS pilots (left to right, Lts. Hurd, Lipscomb, and Guarino) perform a delicate balancing act with no apparent support. Guarino, who flew with the 31st during the winter of 1943-44, stayed in the service. He was later shot down over Vietnam and remained a prisoner of the North Vietnamese at the "Hanoi Hilton" for more than seven years.

The fighter was declared "Category E" (the RAF term for totally destroyed; an aircraft declared such was written off in official records) and a replacement was promptly fitted out in the same manner. Almost immediately a similar 20 mm strike made a mess of the right side of the fuselage, but once again the armor plate did its job perfectly. Fleming's luck would hold out during an even more traumatic mission the following summer.

A mixture of good and ill fortune occurred on the 15th. Lt. Cobb, who was flying an airfield protection patrol, stalked a Bf 109 back to Sbeitla and caught it as it was strafing a jeep; a full broadside from fifty yards at zero deflection sealed the Messerschmitt's fate, and it blew up on striking the ground. Later during an escort mission, several Fw 190s ambushed the Group and took out Lt. Mosby (308th FS). However Mosby managed to force-land his aircraft and returned to Thelepte the same evening.

Indifferent weather throughout March restricted activities, but a steady run of victories was registered, along with several losses. A major change in tactics occurred around the middle of the month. Previously (and like their Luftwaffe opponents), USAAF fighters had been primarily tasked with ground support duties, which precluded any real prospect of their getting at the Luftwaffe, either in the air or on the ground. However, Gen. George Patton seems to have been persuaded that achieving air superiority would benefit the Allied cause more in the long run.

On 21 March the 309th FS downed three Ju 87s. Two days later Lt. N. G. Early (309th FS) went MIA over El Guettar, and Fl. Off. Carver took hits from one of several Bf 109s that bounced his formation but managed to glide back over the Allied lines for a safe crash-landing. Flak disabled Lt. Wolfe's fighter on the fourth mission; he managed a successful belly landing behind friendly lines, but he injured his back when the Spitfire nosed over and subsequently required hospital treatment. Capt. Hill scored his second kill, an Fw 190, over Faid Pass on the 25th.

April 1943 opened on a neutral note for the Group as a whole. A reconnaissance mission on the 1st ran into an equal number of Bf 109s — twelve — over El Guetter. In the ensuing melee, Maj. Avery added a Bf 109 to the squadron's score, and Lt. Corrigan damaged another. In turn, Lt. O'Brien was seen to go spinning down in flames without bailing out, Lt. Peebles was forced to crash land, and both Capt. Banbury and Lt. Brunasky suffered heavy damage to their aircraft. The 309th FS lost Lt. Strole and Lt. Juhnke, both of whom were later

This Savoia-Marchetti S.M.79 is probably the aircraft in which an Italian delegation arrived at Termini at the beginning of September 1943 to discuss with Gen. Eisenhower their country's surrender terms.

confirmed killed in action. Maj. Thyng and Lt. S.O. Kelly (309th FS) both shot down Bf 109s, and claims for an additional three enemy aircraft damaged and three probables were submitted by other pilots.

On 2 April the sole mission was escorting A-20s striking La Fauconnerie. A flight of Bf 109s that tried to bounce the force was initially held at bay, Lts. Huntington (307th FS) and Meldeau (309th FS) scoring one Bf 109 each. However, one A-20 was badly crippled by flak over the target and lagged behind. In spite of continuing cover, the straggler was shot down, no parachutes being seen emerging.

April saw the introduction within the Group of the highly rated Spitfire Mk. IX. Fitted with a two-stage supercharged Merlin 61 engine, the Mk. IX was more than able to combat the Luftwaffe fighters — especially the Fw 190 — whose overall margin of superiority over the Spitfire Mk. V had become ominously clear, at least in the skies over northwest Europe. Its performance advantage notwithstanding, the Mk. IX's appearance was so nearly identical to that of the Mk. V that many Fw 190 pilots were lured into combat with what they thought would be "easy pickings," only to be greatly surprised, often fatally.

A move to Djilma took place between the 5th and 7th as the advance of the ground forces toward Cape Bon against Rommel's exhausted remnants took on full momentum. The previous day, Lt. Fields (307th FS) had increased the Group's tally by one Bf 109. Hardly were the Group settled in, however, when yet another transfer to Le Sers was ordered on the 12th. During the move to Le Sers, three pilots went MIA on successive days. Lt. B. Roche (307th FS) went down during a mission to La Fauconnerie, and the same target claimed Lt. J. Klass (also 307th FS) and Lt. Don Miller (308th FS). All three pilots survived as POWs. Air activity was minimal in the ensuing few days, confined to sweeps and escort missions. An escort mission on the 17th saw the Group escorting B-17s for the first time.

During a freelance patrol to Karouran on the 19th, Capt. Johnson (308th FS) gained the upper hand on a Bf 109, while a sweep on the 21st resulted in no less than seven kills. The 307th led the way with Lt. J. H. White shooting down a brace of Bf 109s and Lts. Hawkins, Wooten, Bryson, and Davies one each, while Maj. Avery completed the list. Seven other enemy fighters were claimed as damaged. Lts. Peebles and Corrigan (308th FS) did not return; there were no reports on the former, but Corrigan was seen to bail out over enemy territory.

Peebles had also downed a Bf 109, but this was unconfirmed at debriefing. It would be a further sixteen days before the facts of Peebles' last mission came to light, not from him but from a fellow POW, also from the 31st FG. Peebles' Spitfire had developed engine problems right from takeoff. He was about to call to say he was aborting the mission, when he became aware of two Bf 109s stalking him from an up-sun position. He turned away and allowed them to close until the leader was about 250 yards distant. Remaining left of the leader, Peebles now reefed his fighter in a 270-degree turn, not only avoiding the enemy pilot's fire, but also directing his fire along the length of the number two Bf 109 as it crossed at right angles. The result was dramatic; a violent explosion around the cockpit of the '109 that blew off its canopy and caused the aircraft to erupt in flames.

In the intervening few seconds the number one Bf 109 had looped and rolled out and down onto Peebles' tail. Peebles' laboring aircraft was unable to outrun the German fighter, and he was forced to absorb the full withering blast of the enemy gunfire. The Spitfire suddenly did a snap roll to the right and fell away. By the time he had recovered, Peebles was too close to the ground to bail out and had no option other than to attempt a high-speed crash-landing. With his harness undone and the canopy jettisoned, it was inevitable that he would pay a physical price. When he came to, he was in the charge of German soldiers, having suffered dislocated shoulders. A doctor informed Peebles that he had been thrown right through the windshield of his aircraft.

Lying next to him in the hospital tent was a P-39 pilot whose untreated leg wound stank with an odor so suffocating that Peebles attempted to exit the tent, but he was intercepted just outside the entrance. Unfortunately his action constituted an escape attempt in the Germans' eyes, and consequently he was shipped out in an Italian seaplane to end up in a prisoner-of-war camp in Italy or Germany. His fellow POW was able to convince the authorities he was unfit to be moved from his bed and was still in the hospital when Tunis was liberated a mere forty-eight hours later!

Next day (the 22nd) the 309th FS was in action. Capt. Hill and Lt. Rahm shared a Bf 109, Hill shared a second with Lt. C. W. Payne, and a third went down before the guns of Lt. McRaven. Capt. Hill, who was currently detached to the 309th FS, scored his third kill (a Bf 109) on the 25th and Lt. Meldeau (309th FS) joined

Sgt. Knack (center) delves into the innards of an uncowled Merlin while Staff Sgt. Lauteria stands on the wing and Staff Sgt. Linder poses by an oil drum. Aircraft has five "kill" markings and is believed to belong to 309th FS CO Maj. Thyng, who finished his tour on 12 May 1943.

(Above) Group personnel inspect the remains of a Ju 87D, one of a number of the infamous Luftwaffe dive-bombers downed by the 31st FG during the course of the North African campaign.

(Above) The cockpit area of Maj. Frank Hill's Spitfire shows five victories to his credit along with the name *LINDY AND FRANK*. Of interest are the internally mounted rear-view mirror and the harness webbing of the parachute pack already placed on the pilot's seat.

(Right) Smoke pours from a burning landing ship, tank (LST), which was beached next to the vessel from which the 31st FG's ground personnel disembarked at Gela, Sicily. Enemy gunfire struck the LST and set it on fire.

in with an Macchi C. 202. Hill's former 308th FS colleague, Lt. Overend, got another the next day while flying in a Spitfire Mk. V. His squadron's second mission this day involved the Mk. IXs of Capt. Johnson and Lt. Dalrymple. On the way back from escorting B-25s, the duo intercepted and spotted two Bf 109s. The Luftwaffe pilots attempted to climb away, but lethal bursts from their pursuers' 20 mm cannons brought both Bf 109s down. Lts. Shafer and McAbee brought the score to five Bf 109 kills. The month's scoreboard was completed on the 28th when Lt. Holloway (307th FS) was the victor over another Bf 109.

The fitting of 90-gallon auxiliary fuel tanks (known as "slipper" tanks) under the bellies of the Spitfires now allowed the pilots to patrol over Cape Bon, but these runs were uneventful. In fact, there was but one mission of note before Tunis fell on 7 May, but it brought great results for both the 307th and 309th. In the course of three missions flown on the 6th, the 309th's tally was boosted by newly promoted Maj. Hill (two Bf 109s), Maj. Thyng (one Bf 109), Lts. Chaddock, Payne, and McCarthy (one Bf 109 each), and Lt. Shafer (a Macchi C.202). Lts. Collingsworth and Hermats each claimed an Fw 190, and these plus Lt. Fischette's Bf 109 added three more to the 307th's total. In addition, four damaged and two probables were reported to the intelligence staff.

The penultimate Group transfer occurred on 15 May, to Korba up on the Cape Bon Peninsula. The personnel found the base to be in poor condition for operations, but the pilots managed to avoid problems. For some this was a short stay, because a detachment was sent to the Island of Gozo close to Malta on the 28th. Those pilots remaining began sweeps over the Italian-occupied island of Pantelleria whose surrender it was hoped would be brought about by an intensive bombing campaign instead of invasion. On the 27th, Maj. Avery and Capt. Taylor received orders rotating them home; Capt. Tom Fleming took over as the 308th's commanding officer.

The Group was by now in the unusual position of operating three distinct types of Spitfire, the Mk. V, Mk. VIII, and Mk. IX. The latter two were basically the same aircraft, but the Mk. VIII bore distinctively pointed wing tips and rudder.

The Allies were now poised to invade the European mainland, although the initial landings would actually be on the island of Sicily, lying adjacent to southern Italy. Crucial to the success of this mission was the capture of the island of Pantellaria, which lay in the Sicilian Straits about fifty miles northeast of Korba. Enemy fighters based there carried out harassing raids on Allied targets, and their low-level approach gave minimum warning. Pantellaria would have to be taken out, either by invasion or by being bombed into submission. It was to this latter end that the Group escorted the bombers seeking to knock the island out of the war.

On 6 June, enemy fighters cut Lts. Mutchler and Trafton (308th FS) out of a returning formation, and their violent evasive action caused them to black out temporarily. Mutchler managed to evade his pursuers and regain contact with the others in quick time, but Trafton survived a nasty few minutes of diving attacks only by breaking into the pack of eight Bf 109s. Three other pilots received permission to help Trafton. As they approached he dived under them at full throttle to arrive back at Korba ahead of the formation!

Since transferring to Korba the men had been able to observe shipping convoys under attack, causing Sgt. Deacon Woods (308th FS) to say, "Boy, they're sure giving that convoy hell!!" He was swiftly disillusioned when a companion yelled, "Convoy, hell — that's us!" In their haste to seek cover some men dashed barefoot across a grain stubble field; their subsequent return after the "all clear" was sounded was much more deliberate! A second attack the next day injured over twenty 309th enlisted men. During one attack, Sgt. Ralph Apple was seen to dash for cover in some high grass and out into the open on the far side! Sgt. Howell recollected looking up as an Fw 190 swept low overhead, close enough for the pilot to be clearly seen.

The lack of enemy action over their airfields in recent weeks had induced a careless frame of mind among the ground crew, but these two attacks provided a salutary lesson in protection and the need for foxholes, especially in view of the fact the weapons dropped were mainly 4-pound antipersonnel bombs. These caused much damage to telegraph cables and telephone wires and gave the ground crew much extra work in repair duties.

It was perhaps some consolation to the enlisted men that next day combat occurred between sixteen 308th FS fighters and an equal number of Macchi C.202s. Capts. Tom Fleming and Dalrymple and Lts. Overend and Wolfe each took down one MC.202 and Lt. Baker a Bf 109. Lts. McMann and Rich were missing on return of the squadron, but McMann was soon picked

(Above and below) Mechanics fit a crane-mounted strap around the tail of Lt. Boardman's Spitfire Mk. V in order to put the fighter back onto its landing gear. In the process of flipping onto its back, the fighter has smashed its fin. The incident is believed to have occurred during the Sicily Campaign.

(Below) Sicilian residents watch as ground crew figure out how to salvage this 309th FS Spitfire Mk. V from amid the cactus bush. The pilot is not believed to have suffered serious injury, although he might not have relished the subsequent discussion with the squadron CO!

25

(Above) Sgt. Petit holds the radio as he helps the helmeted Sgt. Burkowski carry out a radio test on their 309th FS Spitfire Mk. V somewhere in Sicily. The small size of the square radio hatch made such work difficult. Code letters are shadow shaded.

(Above) Lt. Weimer (309th FS) stands in front of a Spitfire, identified as a Mk. VIII by the combination of tropical air filter unit and six exhaust stubs, at Castel Volturno in 1943-44. "Slipper" drop tank is in position aft of the air filter.

(Above) The Luftwaffe abandoned a number of airworthy Messerschmitt Bf 109s during its North African and Sicilian retreat. This example was painted overall sand yellow with U.S. markings. It was test-flown by group personnel, but a sharp lookout was always kept for friendly fighters!

(Above) Its cockpit and engines covered against the autumn weather, a Caproni Ca 211 reconnaissance bomber is seen at one of the group's Italian bases after the Italian surrender, as indicated by the Co-Belligerent insignia on the aircraft's fuselage. The Italian Co-Belligerent Air Force (Aeronautica Cobelligerante del Sud), whose pilots flew with the Allies, was formed in Southern Italy in October 1943.

(Left) The German counterpart to the Allies' Hadrian and Horsa gliders was the Gotha Go 242, which had rear-loading doors and a sturdy tricycle landing gear. This one on Gozo Island, 2 July 1943, was taken over by U.S. units in Sicily or Italy.

These six happy 309th FS pilots have every reason for their joy: On 7 December 1943 they knocked down six enemy fighters without loss. Two of these fell to Lt. Ainley (front row, second from left) and two to squadron CO Maj. Garth Jared (front row, second from right). Jared commanded the squadron from 9 November until his death in action on 18 April 1944.

up out of the water. Rich was initially posted MIA, but two days later was delivered back at Korba. He had been located in his raft, and while an umbrella of Spitfires hovered above, a Walrus seaplane bearing Lt. Mosby sat down and hauled him out. During the day's operations, the 307th and 308th had both added five more kills to their tally, but the 308th lost Lt. M. P. Smith in unknown circumstances.

The previous day Lt. Gooding (307th FS) had been shot down in a tragic case of misidentification. A P-40 of the 99th FS attached to the 33rd FG swung in behind him, and although Gooding waggled his wings in recognition, this did not prevent a lethal burst of fire from the P-40 from blowing him out of the sky. Pantellaria's defenders surrendered the next day (11 June), the first occasion in which air power had achieved such a course of action unaided by ground forces.

On 2 June a number of personnel had attended at Grombalia to listen to Prime Minister Winston Churchill and Foreign Secretary Anthony Eden deliver speeches; the general opinion was that Eden was the better speaker! An even more momentous event was the visit of King George VI to Grombalia on 19 June.

Toward the end of June, preparations were made for departure from North Africa, the destination being Malta's twin island, Gozo.

From here the Group would assist in Operation Husky, the invasion of Sicily. A flying field had been hastily bulldozed out, creating an odd situation in which one runway was slightly higher than the other. As the pilots were departing on the 30th, five replacement pilots arrived to join the 308th FS. One was Lt. Molland, who would ultimately rise to command the squadron. The others, Lts. Roche, Rodmyre, Van Ausdell, and Schult, were all Minnesotans who had succeeded in remaining together since enlisting!

Tragedy attended Lt. Steven's arrival at Gozo; after he overshot his initial approach, he was seen to veer downward to crash in the sea, and no trace of him or his aircraft was ever found. Much more fortunate was another 308th FS pilot, Lt. Fardella. Sgt. Ralph Francis recalls, "The approach area to one of the runways was painted white with the pilots being advised to land behind this section which was at a lower level than the runway itself. Fletcher [Radio Section[and I were working on WZ-Z when three members of an RAF Servicing Commando came along. They said they were responsible for servicing the Spitfire and took over." Francis and Fletcher had crossed the runway when Fardella made his approach in HL-W. He touched down in the white area, bounced forward and struck WZ-Z. A tremendous ball of fire enveloped the two aircraft.

Fardella's aircraft split in two, and Fardella was catapulted some 100 yards while still strapped to his seat. All three RAF crewmen were killed outright, and it was assumed that Fardella had suffered the same fate. Incredibly, the men who went over to recover his body found him very much alive, although his face was dreadfully pockmarked with gravel.

The Group's aircraft had all reassembled on Gozo within a week, and operations commenced on 6 July. A bad start was made on the day's second mission. Combat with twelve Bf 109s or Fw 190s resulted in no victories. Worse still, Capt. Fleming (308th FS CO) was seen to go down in flames, and Lt. Babcock was missing. Babcock had been going on his first mission, and as crew chief Ed Leclair was strapping him in, he had shared his pilot's delight at the news of his wife giving birth to their first child. Babcock did turn up after a few days. He had become disoriented after the vicious combat, during which he was hounded by several Bf 109s, and was short of fuel when he spotted the tiny island of Linosa. He crash-landed and only came round a day or so later in the house of some islanders. An A-36 pilot attempting a landing was killed in the process, and Babcock helped bury him. He then signaled a passing British warship and paddled out in his raft to be picked up; he later rejoined the Group at Ponte Olivo.

Two more pilots did not return with their aircraft. On 10 July Lt. J. Johnson (307th FS) was reported missing but returned later, having force-landed on a beach due to an oil leak. Lt. Conley bailed out of his Spitfire into the sea but was picked up by one of the invasion fleet. This was the latest such incident in Conley's career; he had already suffered two forced landings, and during Operation Torch had been held as a prisoner of the French for two days at Oran.

With the invasion of Sicily well under way, the 308th FS had better fortune on the 11th when Capt. Paulk and Lts. Callender and Waltner shot down three Do 217s from among a force of around twenty. A pair of kills apiece went to the other two squadrons. Capts. Wooten and Winkler claimed Fw 190s, Maj. Hill and Capt. Chandler shared a Ju 88 between them, and Capt. Payne clobbered a Bf 109. The sortie total of 138 on 11 July was exceeded by seven the next day, but with sparse results, only Capt. Collingsworth (307th FS) latching onto and downing an errant Bf 109 over Ponte Olivo.

Staff Sgt. Vaughan unplugs the "trolley ack" from Lt. John Fawcett's Spitfire Mk. IX as the engine is gunned to move the fighter out of its dispersal. Lt. Fawcett completed his tour in late March 1944 just as the Group was converting to P-51s.

(Above) This Spitfire Mk. VIII of the 308th FS has suffered a collapse of its right main landing gear, which has caused the wooden propeller to strike the ground and splinter its tips. The tapered wingtips of this Spitfire variant are clearly visible. Well-tanned torsos of the ground crew suggest this incident took place in North Africa. (Below) The fighter has been raised and landing gear lowered.

On 14 July the Group's aircraft transferred to Ponte Olivo. The ground echelons still remaining in Tunis had been loaded on LSTs on 12 July and had joined up with the main invasion convoy. Although the airfield at Ponte Olivo was earmarked for the 31st FG, its capture and clearance were not realized on D-Day.

As one of the LSTs was beaching, its companion was struck by bombs and set on fire. A 308th FS mechanic, Sgt. Niles Howell (known as "Hollywood" Howell for his home movie camera) was later awarded the Silver Star for assisting in dragging personnel from the stricken vessel out of the water.

The men based on Gozo were flown on C-47s to Licata around the 14th and from there staged to Ponte Olivo to join up with the LST contingent, the airfield having finally been secured after the defenders surrendered that same day. In what turned out to be a fortunate decision, Group CO Col. Dean deemed the main barracks block unfit for immediate habitation. The men accordingly had to pitch their pup tents, which provided minimal comfort. However, any grumbling about their discomfort must have been totally silenced when a subsequent enemy bombing raid set the barracks on fire.

(Above) Maj. Jared has now donned his flying helmet and is ready for start-up. The enlisted man standing on the wing is Tech. Sgt. Ed Waldron, one of Maj. Jared's ground crew. Names of pilot and ground crew appear in the rectangle painted below the windshield.

(Above) Maj. Jared pulls on his flying gloves and prepares to climb into his well-worn Spitfire. The seat belt hangs over the cockpit door panel, which is missing the emergency escape crowbar usually found inside. The Spitfire's fuselage insignia has no border.

(Below) Two Red Cross women dispense coffee and doughnuts to a group of 309th FS pilots. Squadron CO Maj. Jared is second from left. Lt. Wilhelm stands between the women and trio (on right) of Lts. Weismuller, Harmeyer, and Stech.

(Above and below) It seems incredible that Lt. Baetjer could survive this crash of his 309th FS Spitfire Mk. V, but he did, only to bale out over Yugoslavia on 16 April 1944, a victim of "friendly" fire from B-24s. Evading capture, he returned to San Severo in June. The final cruel twist to his combat career occurred on 26 June when he was again went MIA but was not believed to have survived.

(Above) A Spitfire Mk. IX of the 309th FS parked on the grass of a Sicilian or Italian airfield. Auxiliary starter unit squats ahead of the right wing but has not yet been plugged in. The red surround of the fuselage insignia has been changed to blue, whereas the wing marking is still to be similarly altered.

(Above) This C-47 sustained fuselage damage in a landing at the Group's base at Montecorvino in September 1943. The pilot managed to complete a proper landing without reported casualties to crew or passengers.

Among the bombs dropped were numerous antipersonnel types with delayed-action fuses. Army Engineers coped with these in two ways. A steel "mushroom" was lowered by crane over the bomb and the bomb detonated. Alternatively, small blocks of TNT were placed next to the bomb and their fuses lit. Despite the presence of unexploded ordnance, aircraft servicing was fully maintained, although some Spitfires had to be moved away whenever delayed-action bombs were uncovered close by.

Drinking water was essential in the stifling heat. However, the need to add purification tablets to available supplies created a horrible-tasting mixture. It was only after some days that good water facilities were provided when the engineers drilled a well. In the meantime, some more enterprising personnel had discovered a large farmhouse whose ground floor held wine casks, and this source of liquid refreshment was quickly tapped. One man recalls that every one of his squadron's tents had a five-gallon can of wine that was constantly replenished!

Among the abandoned enemy aircraft found at Ponte Olivo was one airworthy Bf 109. The fighter was painted yellow overall and U.S. markings applied while an SCR-522 unit replaced the German radio. Starting the Messerschmitt tested the mechanics' muscles, as they were not used to hand-cranking engines, necessary to start the Bf 109. Maj. Hill was first to take it aloft when he flew over to Aggrigento. When he landed, the brakes did not operate on touch-down, and Hill ran into an earth bank at the runway end where the Messerschmitt nosed over. Damage was minimal, even to the

(Below) Not so fortunate were the objects that the C-47 struck, namely two 309th FS Spitfires, the rear fuselages of which were thoroughly mangled along with their cockpit frames. One fighter bears double aircraft identification letters, a feature of this particular squadron.

(Above) The Spitfire Mk. IX assigned to 309th FS CO Maj. Jared, seen at Pomigliano in January 1944 shortly before the Group moved to Castel Volturno. In common with those of many 31st FG COs, the aircraft letters are the major's initials.

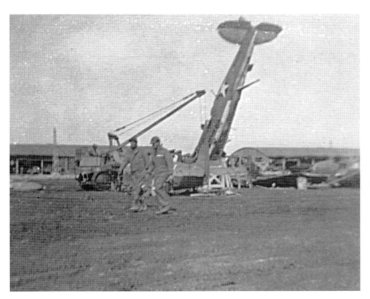

(Above) Two ground personnel walk past a wrecked Royal Navy Seafire, the fuselage of which is suspended from a mobile crane's jib amid the fuselage sections of other wrecked Spitfires. The suspended Seafire displays American national markings as specified for Operation Torch, and its arrester hook is deployed. Photo believed taken at La Senia.

(Above) While based at Pomigliano, the 31st FG shared the airfield with an A-36 group whose primary task was dive-bombing. This A-36 displays the distinctive shape of its Allison engine cowling and top-mounted carburetor air scoop as well as the four wing-mounted .50-caliber machine guns with their bulged wing fairings.

(Below) This Spitfire Mk. IX, flown by Lt. John Fawcett, 309th FS, was the third aircraft to bear the name of his wife. It is parked on pierced steel planking (PSP) in the dispersal area of what is probably Castel Volturno or San Severo. The fully castoring tail wheel is reversed. An open fuselage inspection panel obscures a portion of the squadron code letters.

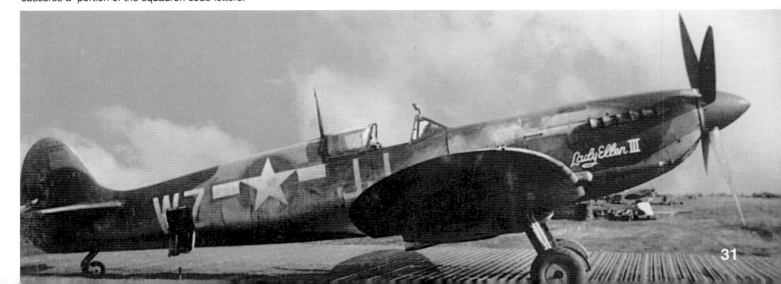

(Above) This Mk. IX Spitfire bears the individual letters "VF" for Maj. Virgil Fields, and was so marked after he assumed command of the 307th FS on 3 October 1943. The rear fuselage inspection panel is open.

First of the Few was the first P-51B received by the 309th FS. The white cross below the cockpit indicated the airplane was fitted with an additional 85-gallon internal fuel tank.

(Above) This P-51B of the 308th FS has suffered a collapsed right main landing gear. Red stripes on vertical and horizontal tail surfaces denote a squadron CO's assigned aircraft.

(Below) This P-51B with a bulged "Malcolm Hood" canopy belongs to the 4th FG, which was credited with one of the highest victory scores within the Eighth Air Force. The 4th took part in the first shuttle mission to Russia on 21 June 1944, staging through San Severo prior to completing the last leg back to its base at Debden, England. The Malcolm Hood was a one-piece bubble canopy, similar to that used on the Spitfire, which slid to the rear. Originally designed by the RAF to give its Mustang pilots improved visibility, the Malcolm Hood took its name from its British manufacturing firm, R. Malcolm Limited. It could be easily refitted to the Mustang by field maintenance personnel.

propeller, and when the Group again transferred to Termini, Capt. Paulk flew the Bf 109 there.

Gen. George S. Patton was not highly regarded within the ranks of the 31st FG. During the Sicilian Campaign, Patton landed at the Group's airfield in an L-4 but parked it so that it obstructed the ready alert aircraft. When Sgt. Al Bleiler came up to him and pointed this out to the general, Patton snapped back, "I'm George Patton, in charge of this whole goddamn island, and I'll park my airplane wherever I damn well please!" The airmen's response was to wait until he had departed the scene, whereupon they pushed the L-4 right back into the surrounding scrub bushes!

Group Command changed while the 31st was at Ponto Olivo. Col. Fred M. Dean was rotating home after serving as commanding officer since 5 December 1942. He had joined the Group at Selfridge Army Air Field, Michigan, after graduation from West Point and had previously served as 308th FS CO. Taking over was Frank A Hill, the Group's first ace, now promoted to lieutenant colonel; his command experience covered both 308th and 309th Fighter Squadrons.

The first of three moves occurred on 19 July to Aggrigento. A bare two weeks elapsed before a second transfer to Termini occurred. Finally, on the eve of the invasion of Italy, Milazzo was temporarily occupied. For the personnel, the living conditions on Sicily were only marginally better than those experienced in North Africa. It would be well into the Italian campaign before permanent and reasonable facilities were secured with the Group's transfer to San Severo.

While at Aggrigento the personnel got their first "taste" of Lt. Edward M. "Jack" Frost's penchant for playing with explosives. The men were just bedding down around dusk one evening when the air was loudly shattered with a series of explosions and flashes. Everybody stood to and crawled into defensive positions, ready to repel a possible enemy assault. An appreciable period of time passed but with no action. Then up from the beach strolled a lone individual, who, on challenge, turned out to be Frost. He had come across an Italian Breda 37 mm gun along a cliff top. He had also discovered numerous land mines on the beach, which he scattered around and used for target practice with the Breda. His comment — "Pretty neat, don't you think?" — probably brought some rather sharp verbal, if not physical, responses from his buddies.

Supermarine Spitfire Mk. V EP17? (last digit of serial obscured by fuselage band) was assigned to Maj. Harrison Thyng, 309th Fighter Squadron's Commanding Officer. Thyng was the squadron's original CO when the 31st Fighter Group arrived in England. The aircraft is in the standard RAF day fighter scheme introduced in 1942: Ocean Grey and Dark Green upper surfaces with Medium Sea Grey undersides and Sky spinner and aft fuselage band. Code letters were Sky.

This Spitfire Mk. Vb was being taxied back to its Kenley dispersal in August 1942 when its brakes failed. The landing gear collapsed while the pilot was trying to avoid a collision with another parked Spitfire. Colors are the standard day fighter scheme. Code letters were Light Grey.

This tropicalized Spitfire Mk V belonged to the Group's second wartime CO, Col. Fred M. Dean. Dean used his initials as the aircraft's code letters in order to quickly identify himself to his fellow pilots. Colors are Dark Earth and Middle Stone on upper surfaces and Azure undersurfaces. Code letters were White or Light Grey. The U.S. national insignia had a yellow surround.

One of the Spitfire Mk. Vs assigned to the 309th FS, EP136 was crash landed at La Senia by Lt. Carl Payne during Operation Torch in November 1942. Colors are the standard day fighter scheme with Light Grey code letters. An American flag was painted under the windshield on the port side.

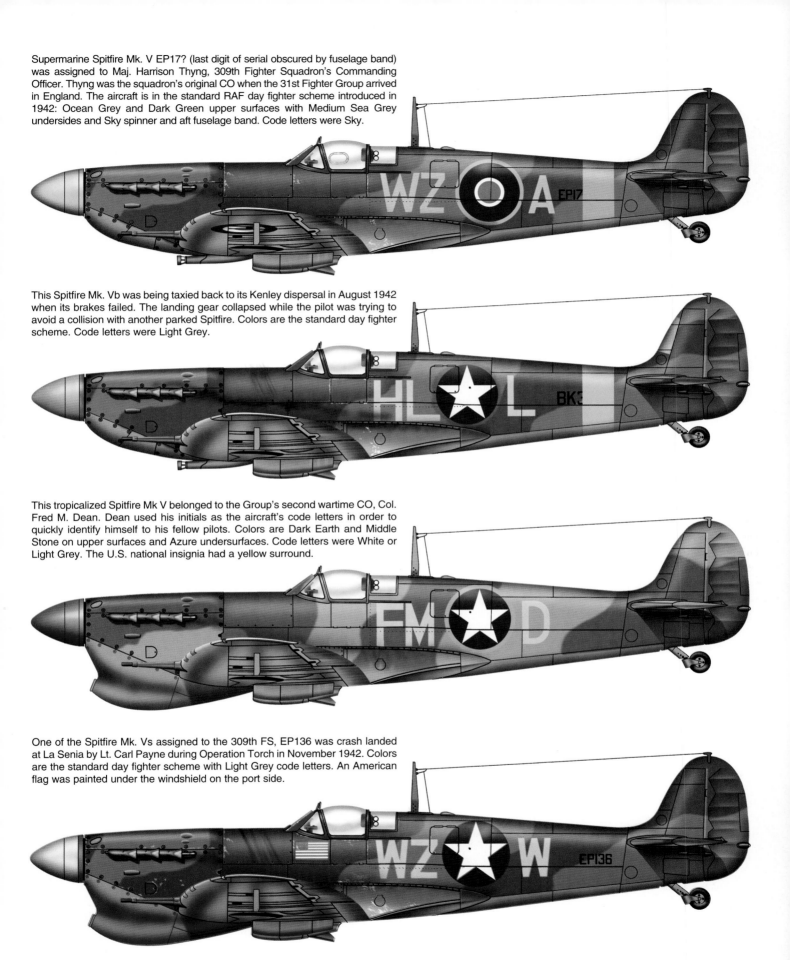

Three A-36s taxi out at Pomigliano, armed up for a mission. Bombs under wings appear to be 250-pound weapons; the A-36 could carry a bomb load of up to 1,000 pounds. The lead aircraft displays a rudder stripe denoting it is a squadron CO's fighter.

An Italian Breda Ba. 25 trainer became a regular Group plaything for a number of months following its acquisition somewhere in Italy. Aircraft carries U.S. national markings with red surrounds and the insignia of the 308th FS under the forward cockpit.

A second dose of "Frost-mania" occurred at Termini, where the officers occupied the third floor of a multistory building. Frost came in with something concealed in his shirt and sat down. Shortly afterward he muttered "Oh, Christ!" as the spinning, hissing shape of an Italian grenade dropped to the floor. The room was cleared in all manner of ways, including out of the windows, but thankfully no one was injured. When the bolder spirits summoned enough resolve to re-enter the room, they found Frost laughing hysterically. His "live" grenade bore no explosive content at all and had only been suitably rigged. Again, his sense of humor was not appreciated.

Combat activity was rather sparse during July but perked up on 1 August when six Mk. VIII Spitfires of the 308th FS tangled with six Bf 109s, Lt. Ramsey scoring a probable. On the 8th, Capt. Paulk and Lts. Heard and Ramsey downed three Fw 190s over Cap Orlando. Capt. Williams' fighter was struck around the cockpit, and he received head and back wounds from which he quickly recovered. Another Fw 190 went down before Capt. Baker's guns on the 11th, but Capt. Williams' ill luck continued. This time he was the victim of flak, and although he made it back to Termini, he required hospitalization for many weeks with the likelihood he would then be shipped back home. Daily patrols were maintained over the Messina Straits up to the 16th after which combat flying was suspended to allow the pilots proper rest and relaxation. This decision coincided

the next day with the land campaign's successful conclusion; the way was now open for the invasion of mainland Europe.

Surrender negotiations affecting Sicily and Italy had actually commenced on 1 August. Lt. Henry Roche and his fellow 308th FS pilots must have wondered about the novel briefing to intercept an enemy aircraft but not to shoot at it! The aircraft in question was an Italian Savoia-Marchetti SM.79 tri-motor bomber bearing the Italian negotiating party, which was duly intercepted and brought in safely. A similar duty to see the SM.79 safely back toward the Italian coast awaited the Group when negotiations were concluded. What the escorting pilots were not told until the mission was completed was that the ammunition had been removed from the guns of their Spitfires to avoid any possibility of an accidental shoot-down! Their reaction to this announcement was rather volatile but hardly surprising, as they would have been totally vulnerable had they run into a hostile reception.

Salerno in the Bay of Naples was selected for Allied amphibious landings with the intent of cutting off the Axis forces as they withdrew northward in the face of the British 8th Army's advance via the Messina Straits. The main airfield was Monte Corvino, and its seizure and occupation by Allied Air Force units was confidently scheduled for D-Day, but the battle was to proceed "according to someone else's plan."

The Group's "piggy-back" P-51D was a war-weary 308th FS aircraft modified to carry two persons. Red, white, and blue stripes on the tail and similar colors for the squadron letters are clearly visible. Passenger comfort was poor, and the noise was ear splitting, according to several personnel who occupied the rear seat.

Maj. "Tommy" Molland in HL-C leads a flight of 308th FS P-51Ds. Eleven swastikas can be seen under the windshield of Molland's aircraft, the only one without a fin fairing. The P-51 at top is Capt. Voll's *American Beauty*, but the pilot of *Waste of Paint* next to Voll is unknown.

The 308th FS was confirmed at the end of August as the main assault squadron for the invasion, and on 3 September, the same day the 8th Army crossed the Straits of Messina, the assigned ground personnel moved into the staging area, where two LSTs had been allocated for their passage. The group's aircraft flew into Milazzo next day to find a dusty and very bumpy runway that stretched the Spitfires' landing gear to their full limits. Some of the Sicilian citizens were extremely casual about crossing the runway when operations were under way. One man's casualness cost him his life. Lt. Rodmyre (308th FS) was just landing when to his horror he sighted the individual right in his path. Unable to maneuver, he felt a thump on one wing but held his Spitfire steady. After switching off the engine and clambering out, he was faced with the sight of human remains decking the wing — the hapless Sicilian's forehead had been neatly lopped off.

The advance party of twelve officers and 183 enlisted men cooled their heels for almost a week before embarking. A change of plan saw the force split between one LST and two LCIs, with the latter casting off first and joining the convoy on the 9th. The LST contingent followed the next afternoon. First Sgt. Elmer Howell, NCOIC (noncommissioned officer in charge) aboard the LST, recalls:

"The captain's announcement that we were going to Salerno evoked the common response: 'Where in Hell is Salerno?' We moved out about 1700 and poked along with dozens of others, taking all night to cross the Mediterranean. It was overcast, and the moon showed pale through it. We didn't sleep much and had to keep lights out, smoking under our coats just like the British sailors. Signal lamps blinked messages back and forth between the ships. At dawn as we neared the foggy shoreline, we could see flashes and hear explosions."

Had the personnel known what was ahead of them, they would have taken every opportunity to sleep, as it would be at a premium over the ensuing period. The shoreline was indeed foggy, but not from natural causes; this fog was created out of battle.

Peaches Beach was barely established as the LCIs and LSTs ground their way ashore and disgorged men and materials. Both the beach and Salerno Harbor to its left were under constant shellfire. The beach was mined, and those mines that had not yet been detected caused casualties among the Allied troops. As one of the LCI parties was landing, a neighboring LST was struck and set ablaze, at which point one man remarked acidly, "This is no place for the Air Corps!"

Despite the general upheaval in the landing zone, the various 308th elements gathered together and worked their way inland toward Montecorvino airfield. They were barely clear of the beach when British officers halted their progress. All around were batteries of field artillery, mainly the lethal 25-pounder antitank gun. Capt. Vostel, in charge of "Buzz" Howell's party, asked for directions to the airfield. The reply was, "It is several miles — but the Germans are less than two kilometers from here!"

The men now retired to shelter in a concrete irrigation ditch where an interior guard duty roster was set up and perimeter guards were posted. Sleep was virtually impossible that night as an artillery duel between the German 88 mm guns and their Allied counterparts split the night sky. German aircraft added their weight to the barrage by bombing the beachhead. A nasty refinement in their bombing techniques was the use of remote-control bombs, which seriously damaged several major Allied warships supporting the artillery with their heavy-caliber guns. Fortunately, the Royal Navy monitors H.M.S. *Roberts* and H.M.S. *Erebus* escaped all attacks, and their 14-inch guns were invaluable in punishing the German positions in the hills, particularly their artillery emplacements.

Montecorvino's early occupation was deemed essential, because Allied land-based fighters were facing flights of nearly 200 miles to provide cover, and the Spitfire's short endurance reduced the time that could be spent over Salerno to a matter of minutes. The Royal

Stanley Vashina (309th FS) crouches by the cockpit of his P-51B. The three full victories and one shared victory shown were his final total when he completed his tour in 1945. He was awarded the Silver Star.

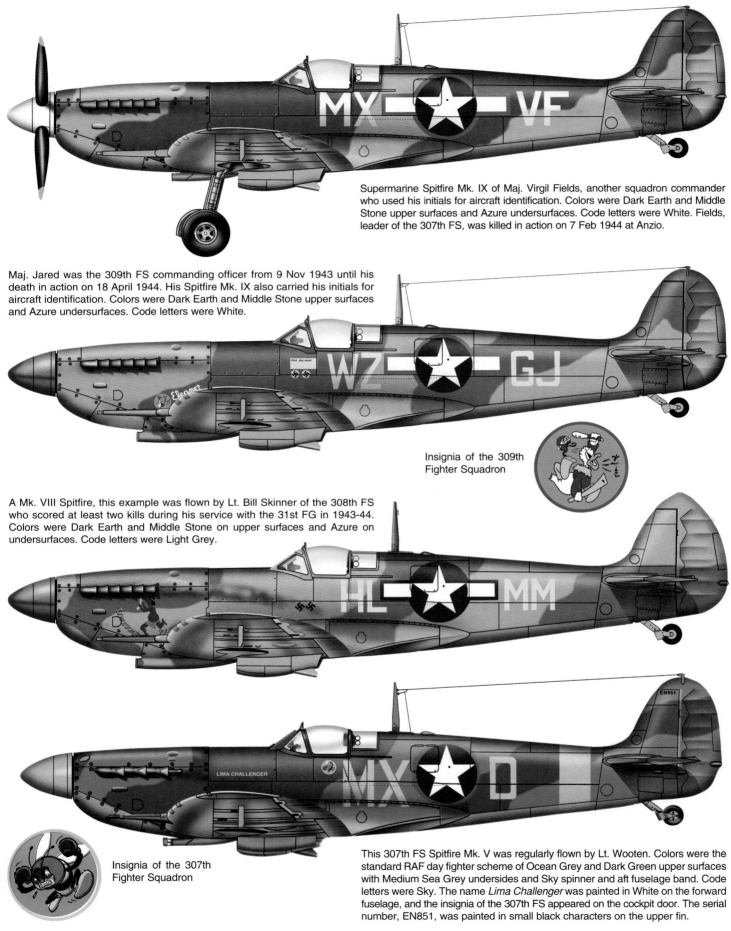

Supermarine Spitfire Mk. IX of Maj. Virgil Fields, another squadron commander who used his initials for aircraft identification. Colors were Dark Earth and Middle Stone upper surfaces and Azure undersurfaces. Code letters were White. Fields, leader of the 307th FS, was killed in action on 7 Feb 1944 at Anzio.

Maj. Jared was the 309th FS commanding officer from 9 Nov 1943 until his death in action on 18 April 1944. His Spitfire Mk. IX also carried his initials for aircraft identification. Colors were Dark Earth and Middle Stone upper surfaces and Azure undersurfaces. Code letters were White.

Insignia of the 309th Fighter Squadron

A Mk. VIII Spitfire, this example was flown by Lt. Bill Skinner of the 308th FS who scored at least two kills during his service with the 31st FG in 1943-44. Colors were Dark Earth and Middle Stone on upper surfaces and Azure on undersurfaces. Code letters were Light Grey.

Insignia of the 307th Fighter Squadron

This 307th FS Spitfire Mk. V was regularly flown by Lt. Wooten. Colors were the standard RAF day fighter scheme of Ocean Grey and Dark Green upper surfaces with Medium Sea Grey undersides and Sky spinner and aft fuselage band. Code letters were Sky. The name *Lima Challenger* was painted in White on the forward fuselage, and the insignia of the 307th FS appeared on the cockpit door. The serial number, EN851, was painted in small black characters on the upper fin.

Supermarine Spitfire Mk. V (Tropicalized) EP837 was assigned to the 308th FS while the Group was in Tunisia. Colors were the standard RAF day fighter scheme. Code letters in White or Light Grey were shadow-shaded.

Supermarine Spitfire Mk. V (Tropicalized) JK836 of the 309th FS had its tail unit totally severed by a C-47 which was landing at Montecorvino sometime in September 1943. Aircraft was painted in the standard RAF day fighter scheme with White code letters.

This Spitfire Mk. IX was flown by Lt. John Fawcett, 309th FS, during 1943-44. The aircraft of the 309th FS carried double aircraft letters in many cases, a practice not regularly adhered to by the Group's other two squadrons. Aircraft was painted in the standard RAF day fighter scheme with White code letters. The name *Lady Ellen III* was painted in White on the nose.

The 31st FG converted from Spitfires to Mustangs in late March 1944. This P-51B was assigned to the 308th FS but has not yet had its code letters applied. Note single yellow band on wingtips. Camouflage is Dark Olive Drab 41 upper surfaces and Neutral Gray 43 undersurfaces.

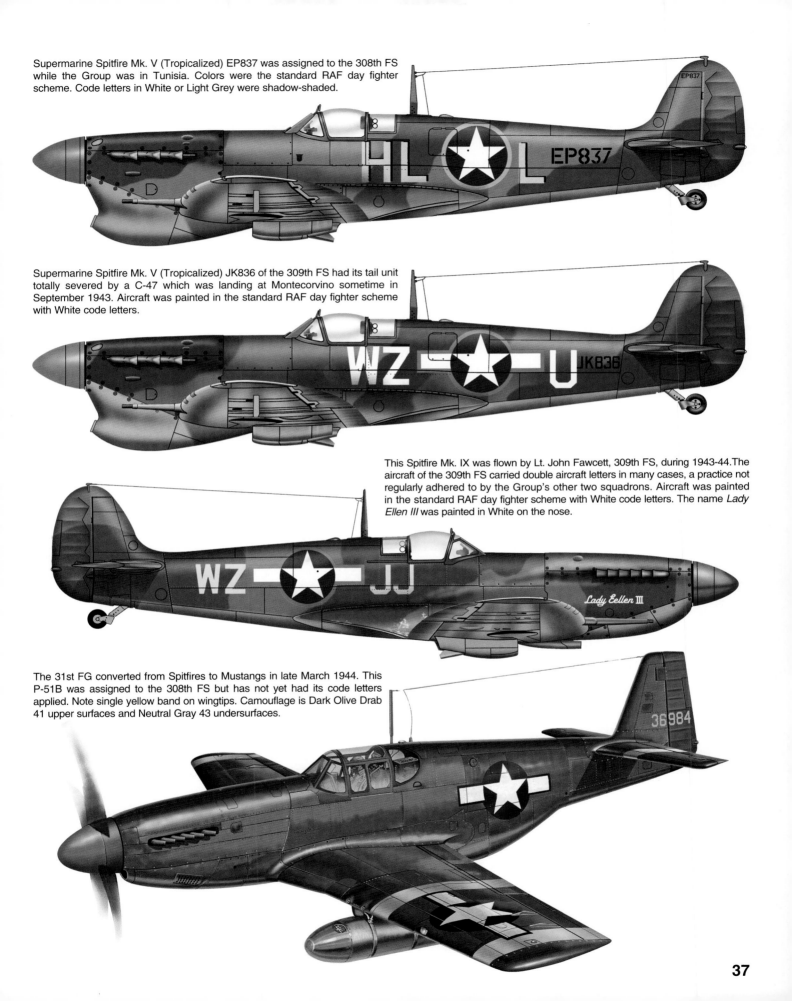

37

(Above) Col. McCorkle carried on the practice of using his initials as code letters when the Group converted to P-51s. The Group marking on the fin has partially obliterated the aircraft serial number. Aircraft in background displays a variation in the positioning of stripes on the fin.

(Above and below) Twenty-one crosses adorn the fuselage of American Beauty, Capt. John Voll's P-51 (308th FS). At the war's end, Voll headed the list of aces from the Mediterranean Theater of Operations.

Navy did have several Seafire squadrons on their escort carriers off shore, but the slow speeds of these vessels coupled with calm conditions were to result in a high attrition rate from deck-landing incidents over the next four or five days. In the meantime, the Group's personnel remained pinned down.

One evening, word was passed around that the Germans tanks had broken through and that a small bridge over a nearby canal was the 308th's specific defensive point. The attack never materialized, to the airmen's relief, as such duties were regarded as the exclusive privilege of the infantry! The 31st's pilots were a regular part of the air umbrella over Salerno, and they soon became aware of the advantageous position their opponents were generally in. It was all too easy for the Fw 190 or Bf 109 fighter-bombers to approach in a steady dive and deliver their ordnance almost before the Spitfires or the P-38s could react to such incursions.

During September, the Group would complete up to six missions daily. These usually involved a mixture of Spitfire Mk. Vcs flying at between 2,000 and 6,000 feet lower than the Mk. VIIIs or Mk. IXs; numbers of aircraft varied between four and twelve per mission. Apart from patrols over the beachhead, cover (known as "delousing" missions) was provided to B-25 and B-26 groups. In addition, there were a few occasions where close escort was given to C-47s.

The Group's combat period over Salerno got off to a solid start on the very first mission. The 307th FS settled onto a Do 217 seen heading inland. Capt. Fields closed with the bomber and set the left engine on fire. He was then forced to break off due to a coolant leak and force-landed near Montecorvino; the Do 217 was last seen heading north at 500 feet. On a later mission, the 309th chased two Bf 109s, but when they were finally in range they were cut out by two RAF Spitfires, which shot down both of the '109s in an expression of Anglo-American cooperation that perhaps was not the best! During the fifth mission, a B-25 carrying Col. Ayling (III SAC) was hit by flak as it was just touching down at Montecorvino and exploded as it reached the far end of the runway; obviously headquarters were still in the dark about the true state of affairs, and several U.S. airmen paid an unnecessary price for higher authority's overoptimism.

During a 309th FS patrol the next day, twenty Bf 109s bearing bombs swept down but left one behind, destroyed by Lts. Hughes and Lupton. Shortly after this raid, sixteen Fw 190s came in, but they, too, jettisoned their bombs when challenged. This force also returned one short, Capt. Shafer being the victor. In addition, Lt. Keith got strikes on one Bf 109's right wing and reported the presence of flames; he was credited with a probable. Capt. Shafer and Lt. Payne also damaged two more. On return, Lt. Webster landed short of the runway, and although his fighter was declared "Category E," he was only slightly injured.

Little combat occurred for the next few days, but there were several incidents among the pilots. On the 11th, Lt. Graham (307th FS) was forced to belly land on Praia D'Mare airfield behind enemy lines. He got out onto what appeared a deserted field and waved. The next day Lt. Lupton (309th FS) diverted into Paestum airstrip inside the beachhead when he lost oil pressure. During one sortie on the 13th, Lt. Overend (308th FS) was forced to bail out over the sea when a main tank malfunction starved his engine of fuel. Lts. Terry and Steger covered him as he clambered into his raft, where he spent an uncomfortable night before being safely picked up.

Lt. Weismeuller (309th FS) and Maj. Paulk (308th FS) added to the Group's total on the 15th. Early in the day, a bomb-carrying Fw 190 was seen at 15,000 feet and pounced upon. The German pilot jettisoned his ordnance as Weismeuller closed to firing distance and sent the Fw 190 into the hills near Montesarchie. Maj. Paulk chased one of fifteen dive-bombing Fw 190s and from seventy-five yards knocked it out of control.

Being an unwanted spare in the formation usually ended tamely with a return to base, but not so for the 309th FS's Lt. Hormatz the next day. On the way back to base, he intercepted a southbound Ju 88. The German bomber completed a diving turn toward the north, but Hormatz expended all ammunition from 400 yards to set the left engine ablaze and send the bomber into the sea.

Two more pilots faced emergency situations during the next week. Lt. Weismeuller bailed out safely on the 19th when his Spitfire developed engine trouble. Three days later, after an inconclusive combat with six Fw 190s, Lt. Rostrand (307th FS) force-landed with a dead engine, the damage being flak-inflicted.

Starting around 14 September, two days of intense pounding of the German forward positions by Allied bombers and artillery allowed ground troops to break forward and consolidate. By 18 September the Anglo-American link-up had been achieved, and the prospect of moving out of the grove of trees into which they had been redirected a few nights previous and on to Montecorvino was eagerly anticipated by the 31st's Advance Party.

The airfield was still within enemy range and being steadily strafed, but no serious casualties were incurred. The nearest the personnel came to harm was ironically at the hands of "friends." Around noon on 19 or 20 September, four P-38s appeared overhead. They were not particularly noted by the men hard at work preparing the base for the arrival of the Spitfires until they tipped over and made a strafing pass at the hangar area!

After the attack, Master Sgt. Rangel (307th FS), a heavyset man, was heard calling for help and was found on the other side of a 15-foot water-filled ditch, having somehow jumped over the massive gap! Unable to swim or to jump back over, he was thrown a rope. However, when those pulling him across realized the water was barely waist-deep in the middle, they jerked on the rope, caused Rangel to tumble into the water. The men quickly scattered as an angry Rangel scrambled out.

Vehicles were at a premium, and the personnel had to scrounge anything on hand. Sgt. Taylor discovered a German command car in a barn. He also found a D-8 Caterpillar bulldozer that was invaluable for runway clearance. Later he borrowed a lowboy trailer and tractor from an engineering battalion.

The first aircraft arrived early on 20 September and were no sooner dispersed than a raid came in; enemy attention, however, was focused on nearby British units, and the Group's full transfer to Montecorvino was free of incident. Beachhead patrols were now supplemented by escort missions for U.S. medium bombers.

One day Col. Hawkins was required to attend a XII Air Support Command conference in Sicily, and Col. McCorkle gave him an old Spitfire Mk. V in which to make the trip. While he was in transit, a message came over the emergency radio channel: "MAYDAY, MAYDAY. This is Hawkins, I'm bailing out!" His engine had quit. Col. McCorkle's immediate thought was, "Good grief! I'm to blame! It was my aircraft!"

Everyone was relieved when news of Hawkins' rescue came through. When he returned to Montecorvino, he was met by the CO, who expressed his sorrow that Col. Hawkins was let down by a Group aircraft. Hawkins responded, "Sandy, the entire search and rescue system around here is under my command. When I called out 'MAYDAY' I wasn't sure what would happen. But I bailed out, landed in the water, and inflated my dinghy. Pretty soon a Walrus turned up, so I took a flare from my life jacket and fired it. They saw it. You know, the only way to find out if a system works is to try it out. Well, I found out it worked just fine!"

Two more missions of note occurred prior to the month's end. The first sortie on the 25th involved the 307th FS being vectored onto four Fw 190s reported at 22,000 feet south of Salerno. Patrolling then at 20,000 feet, the squadron now climbed 2,000 feet for the perfect bounce. Lt. Johnson selected one Fw 190 and poured fire into it from 200 yards. The fighter burst into flames, and the pilot jumped. A second was pursued almost to ground level, but no claim was entered.

Col. McCorkle, while leading five Mk. V Spitfires on the 30th, ran across a Messerschmitt Me 410. Strikes from 300 yards caused the left engine to stream coolant. One of McCorkle's cannons jammed at this point, but further hits brought forth dark smoke as the German pilot weaved evasively while losing height to around

This is an early example of the P-51D assigned to the Group. Although no codes are yet applied, the fighter bears a single red stripe on the fin, which denotes a squadron CO's aircraft.

A P-51B from an unidentified squadron of the Group holds position off the camera plane's left wing. The dorsal fin fairing was only fitted to some late production batches of this Mustang variant.

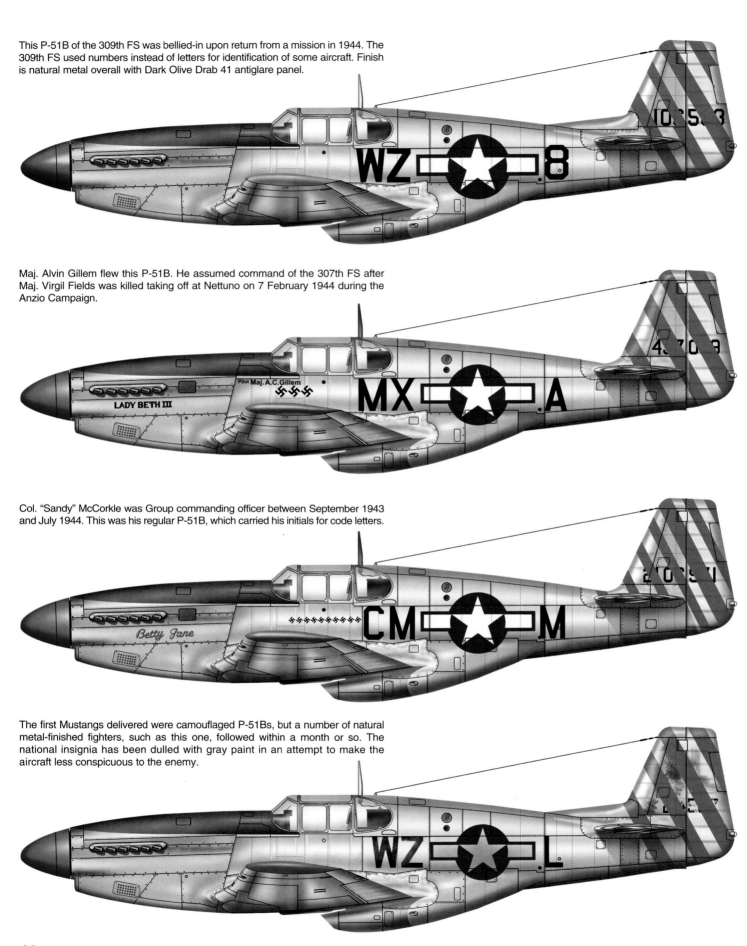

This P-51B of the 309th FS was bellied-in upon return from a mission in 1944. The 309th FS used numbers instead of letters for identification of some aircraft. Finish is natural metal overall with Dark Olive Drab 41 antiglare panel.

Maj. Alvin Gillem flew this P-51B. He assumed command of the 307th FS after Maj. Virgil Fields was killed taking off at Nettuno on 7 February 1944 during the Anzio Campaign.

Col. "Sandy" McCorkle was Group commanding officer between September 1943 and July 1944. This was his regular P-51B, which carried his initials for code letters.

The first Mustangs delivered were camouflaged P-51Bs, but a number of natural metal-finished fighters, such as this one, followed within a month or so. The national insignia has been dulled with gray paint in an attempt to make the aircraft less conspicuous to the enemy.

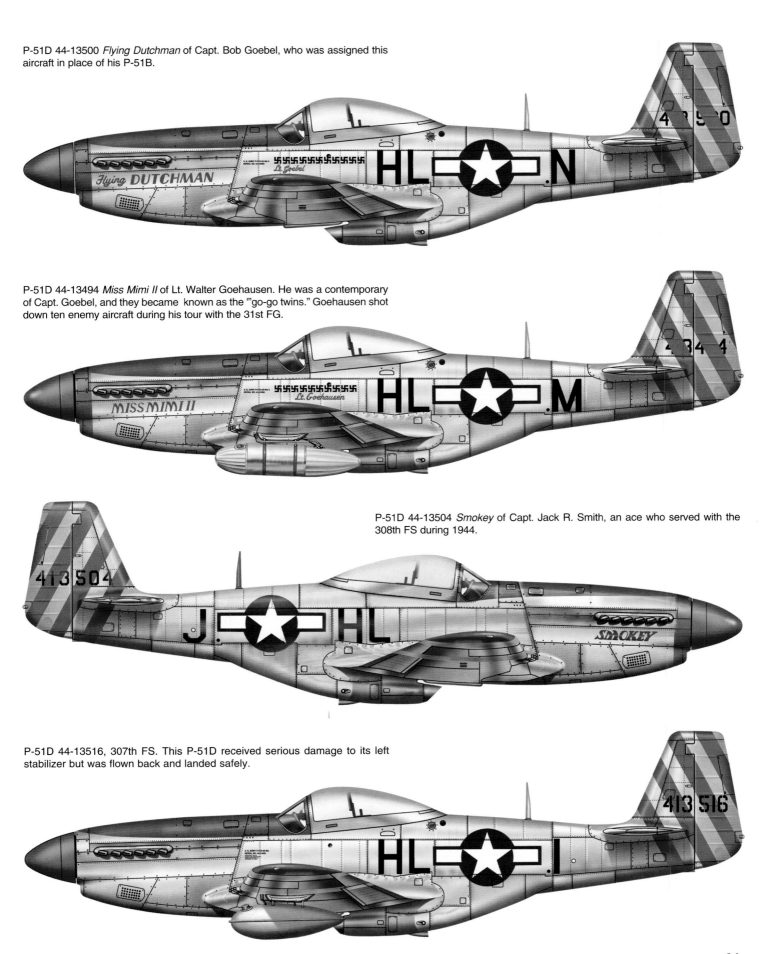

P-51D 44-13500 *Flying Dutchman* of Capt. Bob Goebel, who was assigned this aircraft in place of his P-51B.

P-51D 44-13494 *Miss Mimi II* of Lt. Walter Goehausen. He was a contemporary of Capt. Goebel, and they became known as the '"go-go twins." Goehausen shot down ten enemy aircraft during his tour with the 31st FG.

P-51D 44-13504 *Smokey* of Capt. Jack R. Smith, an ace who served with the 308th FS during 1944.

P-51D 44-13516, 307th FS. This P-51D received serious damage to its left stabilizer but was flown back and landed safely.

Tech. Sgt. Galloway of the 309th FS with mascot "Purp," whose diminutive body dangles half out of the pocket of the sergeant's coverall trousers. Such pets were a regular feature at most airfields.

Two charismatic characters of the 308th FS were Majors "Tommy" Molland (left) and "Stick" Thorsen (right). Both commanded the squadron — in Thorsen's case, twice (8 February to 24 June 1944 and 9 May to August 1945). Molland's command spanned 28 July to 4 December 1944. Both were killed after World War II, Molland dying in an F-82 over Korea.

3,000 feet. McCorkle then broke off as his ammunition was spent and flak was coming up. As he left, fires were seen on the '410, and he was later granted a probable.

There was little further contact with the Luftwaffe to be realized before the Group moved north to Pomigliano. Bad weather cancelled all flying on several days. The general monotony was broken by visits from Gen. Mark Clark (commanding U.S. Fifth Army) and Col. "Shorty" Hawkins, the Group's first commanding officer in the MTO, who was on hand to present Air Medals. He received a heartfelt reception.

Pomigliano was taken over during the second week in October by the ground echelons, who prepared the way for the pilots to fly in on the 13th and 14th. The airfield was adjacent to the Alfa Romeo aircraft plant, but most of its buildings had been flattened by B-24s. The men occupied apartment blocks near the airfield. It was a novelty for the men to sleep in properly constructed buildings supplied with electricity and running water, as the last occasion for the vast majority had been away back at La Senia. Naples was only eight miles distant, and off-duty personnel regularly made visits.

Combat sorties from Pomigliano consisted mainly of patrols over Naples and the bomb line. The initial opposition came from flak, as Lt. Mutchler discovered on one sortie. His aircraft was thrown upward, and he limped home at reduced power with a rough engine. On landing, he discovered one propeller blade shortened and the oil tank hanging on by its tubing! A "probable" claim was granted Lt. Brown during a 307th FS patrol over the Volturno. Two Fw 190s were seen and attacked as they dived away. Brown closed to 200 yards on one, and his gunfire hit the '190's engine and fuselage to bring forth smoke and flame. At a range of seventy-five yards and an altitude of 1,000 feet, he broke away due to the hilly terrain, but was sure the Fw 190 did not pull out. Capt. Fields pursued the other Fw 190, but it climbed away into the cloud.

November opened with a rare combat when six Spitfire Mk. Vcs of the 308th were vectored on to fifteen bomb-laden Fw 190s and Bf 109s. Lt. Brunasky damaged one, and Lt. Woods scored a "probable" when the Fw 190 he was chasing disappeared into cloud, and a flash of flame and smoke was seen on the ground soon after. By this stage of the Italian campaign, cover was being given to A-36 dive-bombers as well as the mediums. Other missions included fighter sweeps as far north as Rome as well as convoy patrols. During one of the target cover missions, Lt. Van Natta (307th FS) pounced on an unwary Bf 109 at a range of only fifty yards. His gunfire disintegrated the Messerschmitt's tail and caused coolant to spew out, whereupon its pilot bailed out.

On 5 November the Group suffered a loss when Lt. Frost (of explosive notoriety) was posted missing. Flak had bracketed the formation, and Frost was seen to straggle, but called up to say all

(Above) Col. Tarrant, in his flight coveralls, briefs the sixty pilots due to take part in Operation Frantic III, the latest shuttle-mission to Russia, launched 22 July 1944.

(Below) Out of his P-51, Col. Tarrant has his American flag armband adjusted by Brig Gen. Strother (306th Fighter Wing CO), who would fly as Tarrant's wingman within the lead flight. The armband was necessary should pilots be forced down in friendly territory.

(Below) Maj. Molland sits at readiness in the cockpit of his P-51D. In a combat career spanning some eighteen months, he shot down ten aircraft with a share in an eleventh. Sgt. Joe Swartz, Molland's crew chief, stands on the left wing.

was okay; sometime later he was no longer around. On 7 November, Lt. Hurd (308th FS) survived a heavy crash landing caused by engine failure, but his aircraft was so badly damaged that it was declared "Category E." To balance the sad news of Frost's loss, word came through on 10 November that Capt. Fleming (308th FS), last seen falling in flames on 6 July, had now been confirmed a prisoner of war.

The next day another survivor went MIA. This was Lt. Fardella, the 308th FS pilot who had survived being catapulted from his wrecked fighter on Gozo. He was last seen in a vertical dive after a scrap between ten Spitfires and ten Fw 190s over Gaeta. Prior to this, he and Lt. Brown had engaged one of fifteen Fw 190s. Brown's fire had only damaged the '190, and with his guns now jammed, he ordered Fardella to take over. As the latter closed on the crippled fighter, he was attacked by two other Fw 190s, but survived the experience to join up with the others prior to his disappearance. A bizarre twist to Fardella's loss was recounted by Sgt. Swanson of the 308th. While on his return from Naples on 6 December, he had met a private from the 209th Coast Artillery based near Gaeta, who stated that his unit had witnessed an Fw 190 being shot down by a Spitfire whereupon the latter was promptly taken out by friendly antiaircraft fire! The circumstances matched those of the mission during which Fardella went missing.

A measure of revenge was extracted on the next patrol when the 307th took on five Fw 190s and Bf 109s. Crossing 1,000 feet above, Lt. Clark blew up an Fw 190 in midair and Lt. Storms shot down a Bf 109, which crashed into a mountainside, after Lt. Adams (who had exhausted his main ammunition while chasing this fighter) ordered him in to finish it off.

Lt. Ron Brown might have added a third. At the start of the encounter he had barely avoided being hit by an Fw 190 as he concentrated his own fire on a Bf 109 and had banked left upon hearing Lt. Adams's terse call to "Break, Brownie!" Brown picked out another Bf 109 and chased it down to deck level and up to twenty miles south of Rome. Coolant was pouring out of the enemy fighter from Brown's strikes, and a kill seemed imminent when his engine suddenly stopped and then restarted. Turning for home, Brown traversed seventy miles over enemy soil at a dangerously sedate speed of 160 mph. He was regularly harassed by flak but sustained no hits. Later examination of the spark-plug electrodes revealed they were all badly burnt or missing. Fortune had proved to be very much on Brown's side.

The Group's P-51s taxi out for the start of Frantic III. Their initial task on the way to Russia would be to protect a P-38 formation making a bombing attack on airfields around the Ploesti oil complex in Rumania.

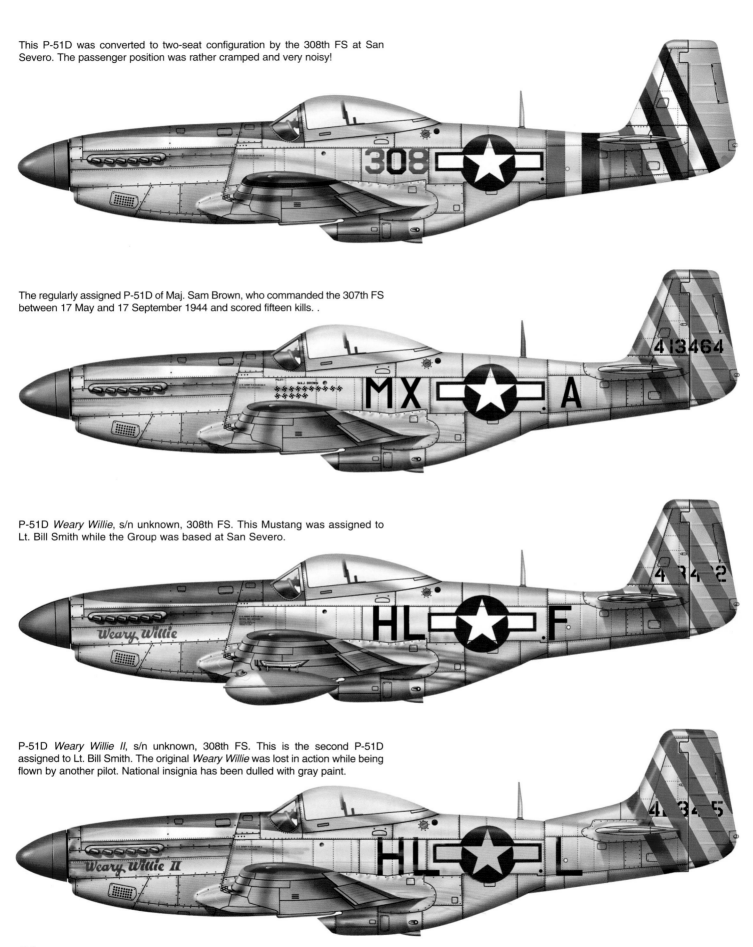

This P-51D was converted to two-seat configuration by the 308th FS at San Severo. The passenger position was rather cramped and very noisy!

The regularly assigned P-51D of Maj. Sam Brown, who commanded the 307th FS between 17 May and 17 September 1944 and scored fifteen kills. .

P-51D *Weary Willie*, s/n unknown, 308th FS. This Mustang was assigned to Lt. Bill Smith while the Group was based at San Severo.

P-51D *Weary Willie II*, s/n unknown, 308th FS. This is the second P-51D assigned to Lt. Bill Smith. The original *Weary Willie* was lost in action while being flown by another pilot. National insignia has been dulled with gray paint.

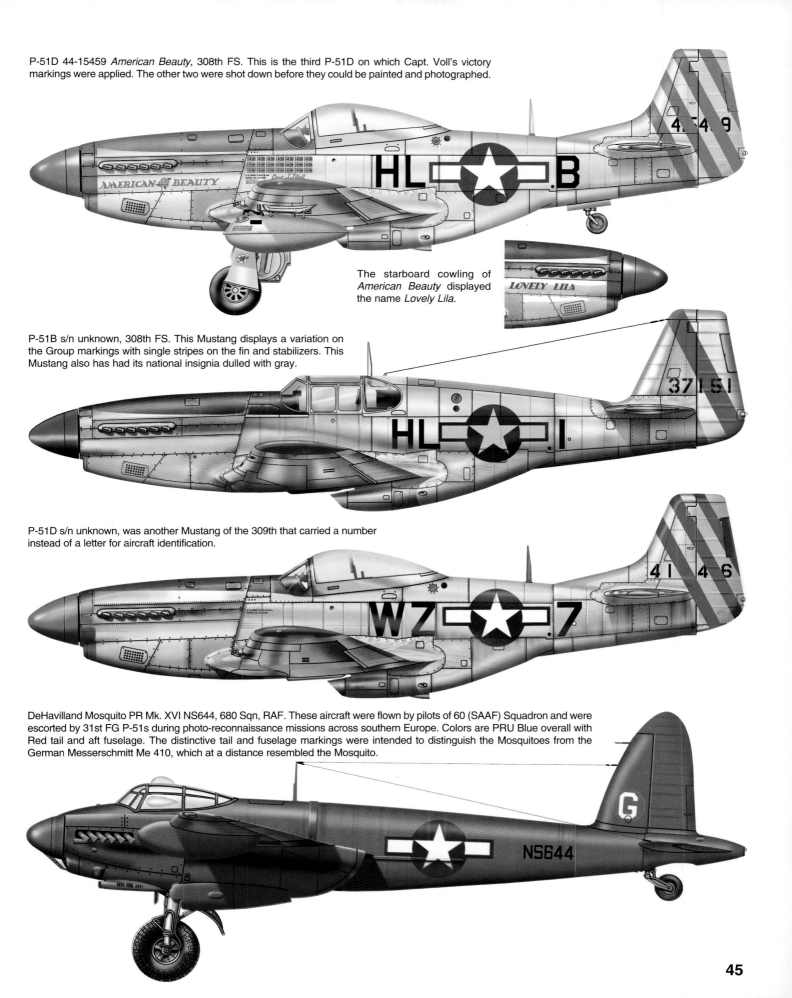

P-51D 44-15459 *American Beauty*, 308th FS. This is the third P-51D on which Capt. Voll's victory markings were applied. The other two were shot down before they could be painted and photographed.

The starboard cowling of *American Beauty* displayed the name *Lovely Lila*.

P-51B s/n unknown, 308th FS. This Mustang displays a variation on the Group markings with single stripes on the fin and stabilizers. This Mustang also has had its national insignia dulled with gray.

P-51D s/n unknown, was another Mustang of the 309th that carried a number instead of a letter for aircraft identification.

DeHavilland Mosquito PR Mk. XVI NS644, 680 Sqn, RAF. These aircraft were flown by pilots of 60 (SAAF) Squadron and were escorted by 31st FG P-51s during photo-reconnaissance missions across southern Europe. Colors are PRU Blue overall with Red tail and aft fuselage. The distinctive tail and fuselage markings were intended to distinguish the Mosquitoes from the German Messerschmitt Me 410, which at a distance resembled the Mosquito.

(Above) During the operation, elements of the 31st FG ran into a force of Junkers Ju 87Gs and downed a large number. This dramatic camera-gun shot shows four of the Stukas; the closest of these is vainly weaving about and beginning to smoke as the P-51 guns are brought to bear on the cumbersome dive-bomber.

(Right) What is probably another Ju 87G is dispatched in a flaming mass by its P-51 tormenter. Group personnel scored no less than thirty-seven aerial and twelve ground victories during Frantic III.

The physical condition of many pilots was by now rather poor, with jaundice and malaria the greatest menaces. Also rife was dysentery, which was the last affliction a pilot making high-speed maneuvers wanted to experience! However, a continuing lack of replacements prevented the Group's doctors from grounding more than a mere handful of pilots at one time.

Despite severe physical limitations, the pilots continued to acquit themselves well. In a sharp exchange with the Luftwaffe on 13 November the 307th's Lt. Hurter shot the right wing off a Bf 109, and Lt. Weismeuller destroyed an Fw 190. Capt. Fields (309th FS) and Lt. Tucker (Headquarters Section) also scored, with Tucker damaging a second. Tucker was forced to outrun two other enemy fighters thirsting for revenge, but this was easy thanks to the performance of the Spitfire Mk. IX he was flying.

The day before, the Group had experienced what would be one of the last attacks on its airfields, current or future. Fighter-bombers dropped a mixture of high-explosive and antipersonnel

Five of the group's P-51s skim low over the airfield at San Severo and into the traffic pattern as the initial pair pitches up for landing on the group's return to Italy from shuttle mission Frantic III, 26 July 1944.

bombs along the northeast dispersal area and the northern perimeter. Two A-36s and a transport were damaged, and members of one antiaircraft battery were wounded. The guns in turn damaged two of the attackers.

The ebb and flow of combat again ebbed when three pilots were lost in six days. Lt. Mann (307th FS) went MIA on 18 November; ground forces later reported an aircraft crashing near the mouth of the Carigliano at a time coincident with Mann's disappearance. The next day it was the turn of his squadron buddy, Lt. Van Natta; his aircraft was hit by flak and was observed going straight into the water with no sign of a parachute. Happily, Van Natta survived. Then on 24 November, an RAF-trained pilot, Fl. Off. Shensburger, struck a building on the airfield with fatal results.

The Allied ground offensive was dragging to a stalemate with the onset of winter. Rain, mud, and snow, coupled with the natural defensive nature of the terrain, was to guarantee that progress up the Italian mainland would be virtually nil for many months to come. However, the second anniversary of Pearl Harbor was an excuse to hand out heavy punishment, even if it was handed out to Japan's Axis partner. The 309th FS added six to their tally, Maj. Jared leading with two Fw 190s. Lt. Ainley downed a Bf 109 and an Fw 190, Capt. Barr got a Bf 109, and Lt. Blumenstock closed out the squadron's account with a Bf 109. Two other enemy fighters were damaged.

The Big Brass hit Pomigliano on 10 December when Commanding General of the U.S. Army Air Forces, Gen. Henry H. "Hap" Arnold, put in an appearance, along with Fifteenth Air Force commander Lt. Gen. Carl "Tooey" Spaatz and Twelfth Air Force commander Maj. Gen. John K. Cannon. Arnold presented the DFC to Lt. Weismueller, and with the press clustered around, asked the lieutenant's opinion of the Spitfire. "It's the finest fighter ever made, General!" was the reply, a statement hard to challenge there and then, as the P-51 had yet to make its debut. Whether the lieutenant's endorsement ever made it into print is unknown.

On 11 December, eight Bf 109s fell on the Spitfire Mk. Vs of the 309th FS, whereupon the top cover Spitfire Mk. IXs joined in. Lt. Porter, leading the Mk. IXs, blasted one Bf 109, the landing gear of which extended before it crashed. Porter chased a second Bf 109 to ground level, and strikes were seen on it, but it was not seen to crash, and he could only claim a "probable." Another Mk. IX pilot, Lt. Faxon, directed his fire onto a Bf 109's left wing-root, but although it fell sharply off to the left and into a steep dive, it was not seen to crash either, so only a "probable" was awarded Faxon.

Two Bf 109s were shot down by Lt. Roche (308th FS) and Capt. Fields (307th FS) on 14 December. Fields and his wingman were diving on six Bf 109s and two MC. 202s when they had to break off to avoid an attack by two RAF Spitfires! They resumed their pursuit, and Fields hit one Bf 109 three times from close range before he had to again break off sharply to avoid the exploding fighter. Lt. "Rocky" Roche was one of ten squadron pilots who intercepted fifteen Bf 109s, half of which were going down to strafe, when they saw their adversaries and turned back into them. Roche's fire plastered the Bf 109 all over its fuselage and wings, pieces flew off it, and the heavily smoking fighter (bearing Italian markings) spun down. At this point Roche's attention was diverted to assisting another Spitfire. However his "destroyed" claim was subsequently confirmed by ground forces, which reported a Bf 109 crashing at the time of the engagement.

Front-line patrols were yielding a steady number of kills. A Bf 109 and an Fw 190 fell to Capt. Barr (309th FS) and Lt. Tucker

On hand to greet the returning pilots was Gen. Nathan Twining, Fifteenth Air Force Commander-in-Chief (left).

Gen. Twining shakes hands with Capt. "Doc" Hardeman (308th FS) while a smiling Col. Tarrant (left) contrasts sharply in expression with Capt. Bobby Riddle (307th FS). Silver Stars were awarded to several Group pilots who participated in the Frantic III mission.

(Headquarters Section) the next day. Barr took out one of three fighters with a long burst. The single Bf 109 that rashly took on the three remaining Spitfires of Tucker's was promptly shot down into the Liri River.

However, the celebrations after the second combat were muted due to three of the Group's pilots going missing. Capt. Barr's wingman, Lt. Walker, was reported to have crash-landed inside enemy territory after calling up to say he was "on the deck" with wing damage and a rough engine. Lt. Archer had called in to say he was bailing out due to engine trouble. Lt. Lyman also bailed out, but he had the fortune to land in a British Army zone from where he was later flown back in an L-4 Cub; he had glided back to Allied lines after his engine was knocked out by a Bf 109's gunfire.

Fragmentation bombs were particularly volatile weapons, liable to explode with the least amount of contact. Therefore, when an A-20 carrying such a bomb load ran into a parked Spitfire during an attempted landing on 21 December, the result should have been a mighty explosion and three dead combat crew. Miraculously, the bomber neither exploded nor even caught fire, although the veteran Spitfire Mk. IX was burned to ashes.

A rare moment of relaxation in the Italian sunshine is enjoyed by this trio of senior officers, each of whom commanded the Group in turn. Col. Sandy McCorkle (left) handed over to Col. Yancy Tarrant (center) on 4 July 1944 after ten months in charge. Col. Tarrant relinquished control to Col. "Danny" Daniel (right) on 4 December 1944.

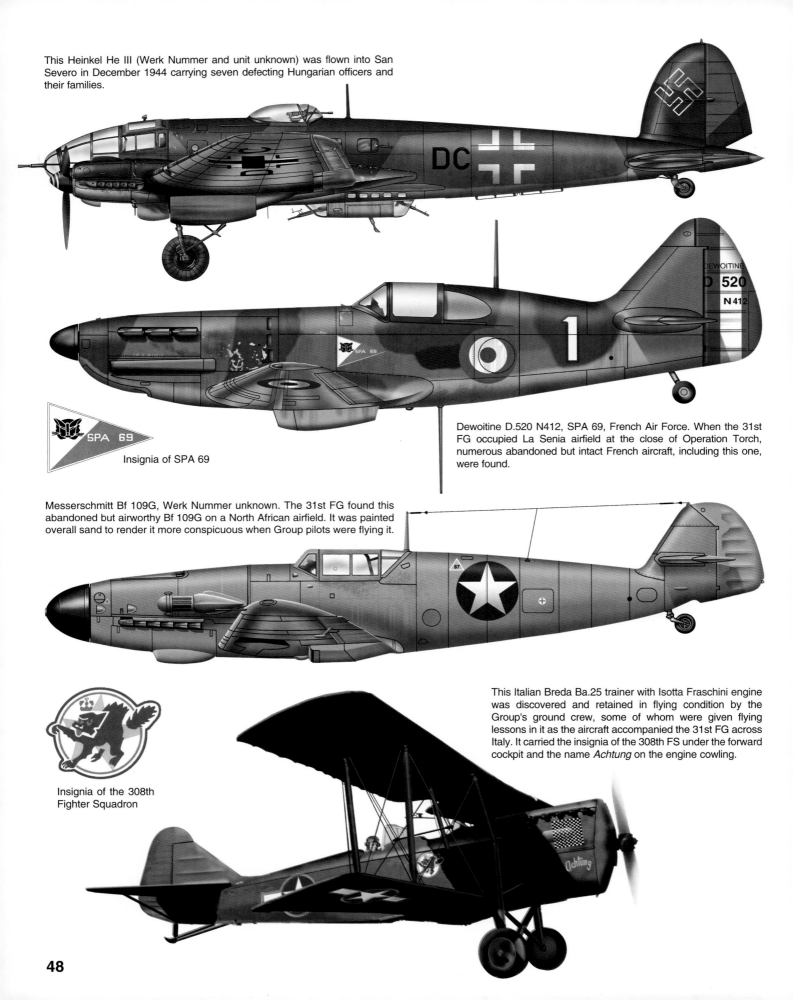

This Heinkel He III (Werk Nummer and unit unknown) was flown into San Severo in December 1944 carrying seven defecting Hungarian officers and their families.

Insignia of SPA 69

Dewoitine D.520 N412, SPA 69, French Air Force. When the 31st FG occupied La Senia airfield at the close of Operation Torch, numerous abandoned but intact French aircraft, including this one, were found.

Messerschmitt Bf 109G, Werk Nummer unknown. The 31st FG found this abandoned but airworthy Bf 109G on a North African airfield. It was painted overall sand to render it more conspicuous when Group pilots were flying it.

Insignia of the 308th Fighter Squadron

This Italian Breda Ba.25 trainer with Isotta Fraschini engine was discovered and retained in flying condition by the Group's ground crew, some of whom were given flying lessons in it as the aircraft accompanied the 31st FG across Italy. It carried the insignia of the 308th FS under the forward cockpit and the name *Achtung* on the engine cowling.

(Above) A snow-encrusted Cletrac parked near the San Severo flight line, which is bounded by several pyramidal tents, during the 1944-45 winter. "Sunny Italy" regularly belied its romantic title, and never more so than during the winter months.

(Below) Winter fun at San Severo. Three officers admire the superb craftsmanship that went into the creation of a snowman (or snowwoman, judging by the contours and hair-do).

(Below) A gun-camera shot of a Heinkel He 111 shows its left engine emitting a solid plume of smoke as the bomber heads inexorably toward impact with the ground. Name of the attacking 31st FG pilot and date of action are unknown.

A possible instance of fuel starvation caused Lt. Gompf to crash-land due to engine failure near Capua on 27 December. In the past few months several pilots had reported engine stoppage at high altitude for no obvious reason, with a restart being effected as the fighter descended. The cause was reputed to be fuel freezing between the carburetor and engine. Usually the situation would correct itself at lower altitude, but engine stoppage was very unsettling to the pilots experiencing it, as they had no guarantee their engines would restart. Lt. Fawcett (309th FS) had such an experience on a strafing mission on 26 November. He was flying as wingman to Maj. Jared over Circeo at 19,000 feet when his engine abruptly quit. Spiraling down and faced with a possible bail-out into the sea, at 3,000 feet he released his harness, flipped open the door, slid back the canopy, and adjusted the trim for a nose-up attitude as he made a climbing turn. It was then that the engine fired back to life, and Fawcett had to struggle to get resettled inside the cockpit, readjust his harness, close the door, and slide the canopy forward before heading thankfully, if shakily, back to base.

The facts of combat life and death were brought home on 28 December, when a shot-up B-26 with burst tires diverted to Pomigliano. Group members clustering around the damaged bomber saw the still form of the pilot brought out; the unfortunate crewman had bled to death from his wounds before proper medical aid could be rendered.

Midair collisions were another eventuality from which there were few survivors. Two exceptions were Lts. Hurst Amyx and Thomas Place. During an escort run on 21 December, the flight leader had called for a reciprocal turn. Amyx dropped below Place's fighter but not far enough, and his Spitfire's tail was sawed off by his colleague's propeller. Both men returned the next day, having bailed out.

The year closed out further aerial contact with the Luftwaffe, with patrols and the occasional weather reconnaissance being the routine. No break was taken even on Christmas Day, when five missions were flown — but then there was little festive spirit in the grim task of clearing the Axis Forces out of Italy.

The first few days of 1944 saw the Group periodically grounded due to wet weather. On 3 January, Col. McCorkle was leading the 307th FS when his fighter took flak strikes in the wing and tail. He was about to turn back for Castel Volturno when ten Bf 109s were spotted. Diving at one he opened up at 200 yards and kept firing while closing to fifty yards, whereupon the '109's pilot bailed out. The first bomb-line patrol of the year on 6 January was enlivened when a mixed force of Fw 190s and Bf 109s was taken on, and Col. McCorkle and Lt. Wes Mckee shot down one each. This excitement was tempered by a return of bad weather, which cancelled flying for the next week.

A second attempt to outflank the German defenses was by now in the final planning stages. Anzio was located to the south of Rome, and an amphibious landing was to be made there toward the end of January. Col. McCorkle was called by "Shorty" Hawkins to the final planning session at Gen. Mark Clark's headquarters at Caserta. At the meeting it was soon made clear why McCorkle's presence had been requested. No other fighter units were marked on the planning map, and there were no other group commanders in attendance; the fighters of the 31st FG were to be given the "honor" of being the first air combat unit into the beachhead.

(Right) An unusual incident occurred on 9 December 1944, when a Heinkel He 111 managed to evade the Allied air defenses and land at San Severo. On board were seven Hungarian service personnel and family members who had fled their country with intent to surrender themselves.

(Below) In this forward view of the He 111, points of note are the spiral markings on the spinners and the heavy-caliber weapon in the Ikaria spherical mounting.

McCorkle selected the 307th FS for the task, after which he commented on the plan:

"I notice that our squadron is scheduled to land immediately after the first wave. Our experience at Montecorvino showed that fighter squadrons on a beachhead cannot become effective until enemy artillery is cleared out, and that requires several days. I recommend we delay our occupation for at least a week. The other point is that our position at Castel Volturno is excellent for supporting Anzio. Consequently I believe that the 307th FS can be just as effective operating from its home airstrip — possibly much more effective — without ever landing at Nettuno."

Sgt "Curly" Carpenter, crew chief for 308th FS ace Bob Goebel, perches upon the He 111's stabilizer.

His words were wasted; the official response was that the presence of the 307th FS on the ground would boost the troops' morale, so they had to be there! Col. McCorkle thanked the staff and then drove back to Hawkins' headquarters, where he complained bitterly about the Fifth Army planners' ideas of air operations.

The Anzio operation (Operation Shingle) commenced on 22 January, and a bridgehead was established in quick order. However, German reaction, coupled with Allied indecision as to whether or not to push on to Rome, left the Allies facing a protracted task over the ensuing four months to even hold on to their gains. It was into this unhealthy position that the 307th found itself thrown. A landing strip close to the beach at Nettuno was the squadron's base. From here the pilots were faced with the duty of scrambling to intercept the Luftwaffe. Radar warning was minimal, and the squadron faced an ever-present threat from being bounced by Bf 109s or Fw 190s. Apart from this, the entire zone was under regular bombardment by artillery, including the infamous "Anzio Annie," a rail-mounted heavy-caliber weapon.

At Castel Volturno the other two squadrons were sending combat air patrols (CAP) to Anzio. This cover system was regarded by Col. McCorkle as wasteful and only marginally effective. As suspected, radar coverage was so meager that "Grubstake" (code name for Fighter Control) could rarely transmit intercepting vectors or even enemy formation heights or positions to the CAP. The best information source was the British Y-Service, which relayed intercepted German communications giving Grubstake basic details about any developing situation.

The average flying time for each CAP was just under two hours, of which about half was taken up in transit. Patrol height was set at between 15,000 and 20,000 feet, but even so, many of the German assaults, which generally took the form of bomb-carrying Fw 190s followed several minutes later by Bf 109s, came and went before effective interception was possible. In addition, the Allied fighters had to devote a proportion of their overall strength to escorting the medium bombers; consequently the attacking Luftwaffe forces usually had a numerical advantage over the defensive patrols.

Despite the German advantage, there were successes for the 307th, such as on 26 January, when the squadron scored two kills with one claimed as damaged and two probables. Another good day was 28 January. That day Lt. Bob Terry (308th FS) was part of a force of Mk. VIII Spitfires led by Capt. Overend patrolling at 15,000 feet when Control called, "Bandits from the northwest." Terry now sighted an Fw 190 well down to his right and already heading northeast. He closed in a dive to 2,000 feet and opened fire

The camera window in the nose and the radio mast relocated on top confirm this is an F-5 photo-reconnaissance variant of the P-38, probably belonging to the 32nd Photo Reconnaissance Squadron. The 31st FG provided numerous escorts for the F-5s of the 32nd PRS as they ranged all over southern Europe.

from 200 yards. Two short bursts produced no results, but closure to fifty yards resulted in hits on the '190's starboard fuselage, after which flames erupted from its engine before it rolled over and plummeted to the ground. During the same combat, Capt. Overend hit a bomb-carrying Bf 109, causing the fighter to explode. Lt. Terry's wingman, Lt. Floyd Redmyre, suffered wounds to his scalp when a flak shell struck his cockpit, but he managed to return to Castel Volturno.

Lt. Terry's mission now had a sting in the tail. As he started home he experienced an increase in engine temperature culminating in thick smoke and flames shooting from the right exhaust stacks. The engine finally quit, and with his aircraft still belching smoke from the cowling, Terry bailed out into the sea off Circeo. He was quickly picked up uninjured by an MTB (motor torpedo boat). These kills were part of a Group total of six, two of which were credited to Lt. Haberle, who did not survive the mission.

During February a steady list of group kills was registered. Col. McCorkle got his fifth kill, thereby becoming an ace, on 5 February when he winged a Bf 109. To that point, only four 307th FS and three 309th FS pilots had achieved ace status. The same day, Lt. Walker, who had bailed out and walked home from a previous mission, was jumped by three Bf 109s who shot up his tail surfaces. He evaded by spinning his fighter down to ground level and headed for base.

Lt. Skinner was credited with a Bf 109 on the 12th. Eight days later Lts. Hurd and Schult each downed a Bf 109. Even better results came from the mission on 22 February. Near Valmontone no less than five Bf 109s and one Fw 190 fell to Maj. Molland (two), Maj. Thorsen, and Lts. Hurd, Brown, and Walker. The cost was two newly arrived pilots. Lt. Hackbarth was last seen trying to bail out of his badly damaged Spitfire while being harried by three Bf 109s, while Lt. Horace Comstock was also killed in action. Squadron veteran Lt. Larry Guarino recalled saying to a fellow pilot some days later, "Isn't it a damn shame?"

"What about?"

"About Comstock and Hackbarth getting killed."

"Who were they?" was the seemingly callous response. The duo had only been four days at the base, and few knew of their presence. Of course, it did not do to dwell on losses, and an apparently hard-nosed attitude was usually adopted in such circumstances. Maj. Thorsen had better luck on this mission after crash-landing just inside Allied lines.

Lt. Elmer Livingston recalls the 307th's service at Anzio:

"We arrived at Anzio to find our runway was a PSP [pierced steel planking — a prefabricated runway material comprised of strips of sheet steel, each approximately 2 feet wide and 12 feet long, drilled with holes for drainage of water, and having tabs and slots allowing them to be interlocked to form a semi-permanent surface] strip very close to the beach which made for tricky landings. We pitched tents, and I dug below ground level to ensure maximum cover from the constant shelling. Foxholes were also dug in number. If not flying, we would be standing by on alert to scramble.

"On 5 February four of us were scrambled to intercept bandits coming in from the north. During the engagement I found myself in a tight Lufbery on an Fw 190's tail. I fired a couple of bursts, and he blew up with some pieces nearly hitting my Spitfire. While I was busy with this, another Fw 190 was shooting my tail to pieces. I spun out after losing control, and then had one hard time trying to keep airborne. Having very little rudder control and with elevators useless, I had to use lots of power to keep my nose up and regain our strip. I powered the Spitfire down onto the runway but completely lost control at this point, and the aircraft went skidding off the runway and out across the sand. It was destroyed but I hadn't a scratch on me!

"By 6 February I noted we had lost several Spitfires through shell-fire. I think it was around 15 February that we moved back to Castel Volturno with what aircraft we had left." (According to Col. McCorkle, the squadron returned with just over half of the twenty-nine fighters it took into Anzio.)

It was bad enough when newly assigned pilots were lost in action, but the loss of a combat-experienced pilot was even more unsettling. Maj. Virgil Fields had come to the 31st FG on 15 December 1942 and had taken command of the 307th FS on 3 October 1943. He was in charge of the squadron while it was flying out of Anzio and operating under the most primitive and perilous combat conditions. The greatest potential risk (due to basic radar warning equipment) was of being bounced on takeoff. On 7 February the first Spitfires were just lifting off, when the squadron was assailed by a pack of enemy fighters. Field's aircraft was struck by a fusillade of shells that caused it to explode, killing the hapless CO. Some measure of revenge was extracted by Lts. Tyne and Moore, who both scored kills in the ensuing combat.

Winter has settled in at San Severo, and snow has liberally covered the ground as well as these 309th FS P-51Ds. The yellow identification stripe on the wing of this Mustang is positioned further inboard than usual.

(Above) Three 309th FS ground crew gather around to await the report of the mission and the aircraft's performance from *Bonnie II*'s pilot Maj. Buck, who seems to be lost in his own thoughts but is more likely just exhausted. Red wingtip paint has peeled badly.

(Below) Lt. Bratton of the 309th FS (left) enjoys a well-earned cigarette following a mission. The P-51 probably belongs to another pilot, as Group records indicate Bratton did not achieve the number of kills shown. Bratton was MIA after the mission of 22 August 1944. Officer on right is Lt. Kello.

(Above) Lt. Jack R. Smith (308th FS), who flew his tour of duty during 1944-45 and scored five kills, stands on the right wing of his P-51D after completing his final mission in late February 1945. Drop tanks still in position under the wings suggest the mission was uneventful, with no enemy fighters encountered.

(Below) A rather bleak Italian landscape provides the backdrop for *Muscles* and its pilot as the P-51D is pulled up off the runway at San Severo. The mountainous terrain within the vicinity of the base could present a mortal hazard to the pilots in poor visibility conditions.

The 309th enjoyed a successful ground-controlled mission on the 13th. Maj. Jared was advised that there were two bogies at 11,000 feet in the vicinity. Lts. Harmeyer and Fawcett were scrambled to investigate and intercepted two Bf 109s. Harmeyer singled one out and hit it, and although Harmeyer was unsure of its fate, Fawcett confirmed that it had crashed. Fawcett, experiencing problems in releasing his drop tank, eased off his chase to allow Harmeyer to take over. Harmeyer made a curving approach on the apparently lax Fw 190 pilot, who paid the price when he was shot out of the sky. The combat complete, Fawcett called Control to say, "You know the two enemy aircraft you reported? Well, they *were* there," stressing the word "were."

The 309th FS was involved in the month's final action on the 29th when three Fw 190s were destroyed. However, this was at the cost of Lt. Nisbet, who was forced to bail out over enemy territory.

On 3 March the Group enjoyed its first twenty-four-hour rest since the previous June, but heavy rain ensured the day's benefits were marginal. By now more missions were being flown to other locations, particularly Cassino, where the Allies' principal ground thrust was stalled. It was over this fiercely contested town that three more kills came the 308th's way. Some thirty Fw 190 fighter-bombers were intercepted, and in a hard-fought combat Lt. Hurd and Lt. Rodmyre clobbered two Fw 190s, and Lt. Ricks downed one of two Bf 109s on the tail of a 307th FS Spitfire. The latest Cassino mission the next day saw Hurd add to his tally with a pair of Bf 109s. These were part of a quartet of enemy fighters, none of which returned to base, as Lts. Jacobs and Guarino duly dispatched the other pair!

March 13 proved unlucky for two Luftwaffe pilots. The pair was reported southwest of the airfield, but before a scramble was ordered, the duo changed course, and control vectored the returning 307th FS onto them. When intercepted, the Bf 109 and Fw 190 dived ahead of the chasing pack, but Lts. Vaughn and Livingston, who had been previously ordered down to low level, intercepted and downed the two fighters. Seven kills were registered on the 18th, including two by the 307th FS; the overall Group score was now 185. Then on the 21st, Lt. Hurd nailed two out of four Bf 109s downed by the 308th FS to raise his total to six.

Taking on unequal numbers of the Luftwaffe was not recommended, but six 308th FS pilots got away with this on 22 March. Lt. Trafton led five other Mk. VIII Spitfires into a bounce of some fifty Fw 190s and Bf 109s. Incredibly, all six returned. Two Fw 190s were not so lucky. Lt. Roche exploded one as it headed up in a climbing turn; three other fighters were damaged. The 309th's Lt. Fawcett completed what would turn out to be his last mission, but as he taxied into his dispersal in the twilight, one wheel went off the PSP and into the sand, whereupon his Spitfire unceremoniously nosed over.

An indication that major changes were in the wind came on 11 November when Col. McCorkle and Lt. Meador flew in with two P-51 Mustangs. On 23 March, Capt. Brooks, a former Group pilot now with the 354th FG, gave a talk on the P-51's capabilities. Most of the pilots present probably felt skeptical about the reputed performance of the P-51, having seen how its predecessor, the A-36, performed. In addition there was an understandable deep sense of

Although dive-bombing was not ordinarily a function of the 31st FG, this 309th FS P-51B carries two practice bombs under the wings.

loyalty to the Spitfire, a fighter that had earned the affection of all who had flown it in combat. However well the P-51 had so far performed over northwest Europe, it would be on trial as far as the 31st was concerned.

Conversion to P-51s became hard fact four days later when five Mustangs flew in from North Africa. These were "razor-back" B-models with side-hinged canopies and armed with only four .50-caliber machine guns. The heavy, flat-roofed, framed canopies did not make for pilot comfort or good visibility, and four guns were not much firepower compared to that of the Bf 109 and Fw 190. Initial conversion flights by the Group's pilots might have given them a more favorable opinion of this improved version of North American Aviation's fighter, were it not for the P-51B's resemblance to the Bf 109, a resemblance that would bring grief to the Group during its inaugural bomber escort mission on 16 April.

The final Spitfire mission was flown on 29 March and was sealed with a kill when Lt. Emery shot down an Fw 190 during a sweep up to Rome. Since commencing operations in August 1942, the Group had claimed 192 enemy aircraft destroyed with their Spitfires. These had been claimed by the 307th FS (65), 308th FS (65), 309th FS (56 1/2) and headquarters (6) respectively. This was far from the total claimed by the Army Air Forces' current top-scoring unit — the 82nd FG flying P-38s — but tactical missions of the sort carried out by the 31st FG were not the best method of engaging the Luftwaffe. The Group's conversion to the P-51, along with its reassignment to strategic operations, would bring about a dramatic improvement in its ability to seek out and destroy its aerial adversaries.

At the end of March 1944 the 31st FG prepared for transfer to what would be its most permanent airfield location during World War II. San Severo lay in the Foggia Plain on Italy's southeast coastal region bordering the Adriatic Sea. In addition to a change of base, the 31st would also be transferred out of the Twelfth Air Force and into the Fifteenth Air Force. The primary mission of the 31st now would be to escort the Fifteenth's heavy bomber groups also based on Foggia Plain. The bombers would range northward to strike at principal targets in Rumania, Hungary, Czechoslovakia, Austria, and southern Germany. These strikes and those of the other daylight force — the Eighth Air Force — would carry out the Allies' combined bombing policy: to smash the Nazi industrial and military potential to wage war. The task of the fighter escorts, in addition to protecting the bombers, was to drive the Luftwaffe from the skies.

This 309th FS P-51B was just airborne when it stalled and crashed. The impact tore out the engine and twisted the rear fuselage, which was totally shattered. Despite the high degree of damage, the pilot suffered only a broken nose, as his face probably struck the gun sight.

(*Above*) Maj. George T. Buck hauls himself out of the cockpit of his P-51D *Bonnie III,* probably near the end of his combat tour, as the kill markings represent his final figure for aircraft shot down or destroyed on the ground. Buck was the 309th FS CO from 12 October 1944 to16 February1945.

(*Above*) The total disintegration of this 309th FS P-51D reportedly left the pilot uninjured. (*Below*) Not so fortunate was a British serviceman driving the vehicle caught in its path. The errant fighter wrought a trail of destruction during its attempted takeoff.

Transfer to San Severo was begun on 3 April. The living quarters were located a few miles away from the airfield, which created transportation problems due to the primitive road surfaces with which the Group's already well-worn trucks had difficulty coping. The pilots continued to train on an increasing number of newly delivered P-51s, and on 14 April Col. McCorkle led the Group in a practice formation to and from Cap Spartivento. By coincidence, a number of pilots who had flown nothing but Spitfires had now finished their tours and were about to leave for home; many had served since the Group had initially moved out of North Africa, and they must have had mixed emotions at severing links just as a new and exciting operational chapter was opening up.

Turnul Severin, Romania, was the designated target on 16 April when the pilots were briefed for their first P-51 mission. Among the rookie pilots was Lt. Bob Goebel, a tousle-headed adolescent from Wisconsin who was destined to make a name for himself in the months ahead. The overall flight distance was 800 miles, and there was no enemy action to disturb the pilots' concentration on flying their new fighters. Two 309th pilots got a lethal taste of friendly action, however. As the squadron weaved over a B-24 formation, their P-51s were struck by fire from the bomber gunners. Lt. Baetjer's aircraft was so badly damaged that he took to his parachute over Yugoslavia. To a nervous gunner reacting quickly in the heat of an aerial battle, the P-51's shape could resemble that of a Bf 109, and that appeared to have been the case on this day. The result was the loss of one P-51 and its pilot.

Among the returning pilots there was now a sense of wonder at the much longer range of the Mustang compared to the short-range Spitfire. There also must have been an equal sense of anticipation at taking on the Luftwaffe's Fw 190s and Bf 109s that sought to stop the Army Air Forces' bombing missions into southern Europe. No longer would Luftwaffe pilots be able to evade combat by diving away, because the P-51 could overtake them, while its ability to sustain turns during combat was almost on a par with the Spitfire.

The ground crew also benefited from the change to the Mustang. Now they could relax after completing their preflight duties, generally secure in the knowledge that just the one sortie would be flown. This was in sharp contrast to previous operations with the Spitfire, which had seen as many as four daily sorties launched, a workload providing the mechanics with little time to relax.

Col. McCorkle drew first blood with the P-51 by shooting down two fighters on 17 April while leading the 309th FS; Capt. Brown (307th FS) destroyed a third. Lt. Demeron (309th FS) was MIA. The mission two days later was regarded with mixed emotions. In a whirling dogfight, Lts. Trafton and Byrnes (308th FS) destroyed a Bf 109 each as did Lt. Loving (309th FS), and three other Bf 109s were damaged. The cost was high; Maj. Jared, 309th CO, was killed, and Lts. Reynolds and Ricks went missing while returning through very bad weather. Maj. Meador replaced Jared as squadron commanding officer.

Distinctive colored markings for the group's P-51s were developed soon after conversion from the Spitfire. Group CO Col. McCorkle felt the standard code letters did not provide him with sufficient identification, and Sgt. Chris Christenson accordingly painted a single red stripe on the colonel's fighter. Soon after, McCorkle ordered all other P-51s to bear a single red stripe as a Group identifier. There still being no separate identification of squadron COs, it was decided to add one red fuselage band to their aircraft and two bands to Group CO's aircraft. Finally, all aircraft had the entire tail section painted with red and white stripes, and thus the Fifteenth Air Force's "candy stripe" outfit was born! (Col. McCorkle had followed his predecessors as Group CO in applying his initials CMM as his aircraft's code letters.). A final marking refinement on all P-51s was the addition of red and yellow wing-tip stripes and a yellow stripe on each wing center-section. Some fighters also bore evidence of stabilizer stripes prior to the introduction of the full Group markings.

The first high-level mission to the notorious Ploesti oil fields (soon to be known as "the graveyard of the Fifteenth") was on 21 April. Ploesti's reputation as a tough target was confirmed when the Group sighted and engaged about sixty enemy fighters. The 308th FS gained its second ace when Lt. Molland shot down two; two other 308th pilots, Lts. Trafton and Hughes, doubled the tally. A further twelve kills were recorded by the remainder of the Group pilots, including a trio by Lt. Ainley (309th FS). Another trio was not so welcome: Lts. Lyman, Jackson, and Williams were all MIA.

The Messerschmitt plant at Wiener Neustadt near Vienna proved to be another well-defended target. Bob Goebel recalled the weather forecast as "bad." Despite his novice status, he was flying as Maj. Thorsen's wingman, with the 308th leading the Group. Another 308th pilot, Lt. Hughes, was reportedly heard to say to an intelligence officer, "G-2, isn't it a beautiful day to get shot down?" These proved to be tragically prophetic words.

Hughes was number two in Lt. Trafton's flight. Lt. Rodmyre of the same flight recalls these two pilots suddenly diving without warning to engage a sizeable number of enemy fighters; both were subsequently shot down; Trafton survived, Hughes did not. On return, claims for two destroyed by the hapless duo were entered as part of the overall figure of sixteen kills recorded for the Group.

To complete a miserable day for the 308th, a third pilot, Lt. Johnson was MIA. Bob Goebel was his wingman and recalled how Johnson jettisoned his drop tanks and turned inside the flight's lead element, followed only by his wingman, to engage three Bf 109s. The dangerously isolated pair hurtled downward with Johnson drawing ever further ahead of Goebel as the vicious centrifugal forces took hold. Recovering from the curving dive, Goebel found Johnson had disappeared, and he now turned on full emergency power to avoid two Bf 109s closing directly ahead before heading home. A fourth loss was a recently arrived 309th FS pilot, Lt. Jackson. In exchange, the Group had removed thirteen fighters from the Luftwaffe's Order of Battle; Col. McCorkle took out two Bf 110s and an Fw 190 himself.

During these early P-51 operations, a Maj. Jim Goodson came on temporary assignment to San Severo. "Goody" Goodson was already an ace with the 4th FG, and during the two weeks with the 31st he added two more kills to his total while flying with the 307th FS on mission of 21 April. What impressed his armorer was the small number of rounds Goodson's guns had used in scoring the victories. His reception from the 31st's personnel seemed positive, unlike their later impression of Goodson's contemporaries, when the 4th staged through San Severo during one of the Operation Frantic shuttle missions to Russia.

A scrubbed mission on the 25th brought welcome relief to the pilots who had flown eight out of the last nine days. The fact that

Two sergeants from the Radio Section of the 309th FS examine the severe damage of a P-51D's center fuselage. The cause of the peeled and missing panels could have been flak or even an accidental detonation of the IFF (Identification, Friend or Foe) equipment, which was considered so secret it carried an explosive charge to destroy it in the event of a landing behind enemy lines.

Flames rapidly engulf a P-51B lying off the runway end after a takeoff accident at Mondolfo, as another more fortunate fighter lifts off.

(Right) An RAF Spitfire Mk. IX standing on its prop gets a close look from a mechanic of the 31st FG at either San Severo or Mondolfo, judging from the Type "C" roundels, which were introduced in early 1945, on the upper wings

(Above) Another prized possession of the 31st FG was this Italian Macchi C. 202. Two men crank the starting handle ahead of the wing, while a third sits in the cockpit. Absence of a cockpit canopy was a feature of this design. Throttle operation of Italian aircraft was the opposite of Allied fighters; power was applied by pulling back the lever instead of pushing it forward.

(Below) The 309th FS's radio truck had a "shell" built onto the basic vehicle structure, and just like one of the squadron's aircraft, carried the squadron's code letters and U.S. national insignia, but with a radio beacon symbol replacing the usual aircraft letter.

Group pilot strength was barely above the minimum needed to sustain operations was an additional strain, as very few men could be rested. In fact it was three days before the Group was to be called on again, and April's books were closed with three consecutive missions. On the 28th, three more kills were claimed. During a long run to Toulon, France, on the 29th, Lts. Molland and Jacobs added to the 308th's score, while Lt. Goehausen claimed another victory for the squadron on the 30th. He had aborted the mission and was near Ancona when he sighted a low-flying Ju 88; a firing pass did not seem to do much damage, but the bomber still went into the water.

Sgt. Lasalle had installed a cigarette case in Lt. Bob Riddle's cockpit close to the throttle quadrant, because Riddle was a three-pack-a-day man. On return from one mission Riddle loosened his shoulder harness, extracted a cigarette, and lit up. The P-51 had a flare chute on the lower left side of the cockpit; directly above it was the flare holder, which in this instance only held a signal flag. His smoke completed, Riddle ejected the butt (or so he thought) down the chute. A few minutes later he became aware of wisps of smoke rising and escaping through the gap of his slightly open canopy. The smoke intensified, and Riddle now saw a glow in the flare holder. Even with loosened straps he could not reach far enough over to extinguish the embers; at one point he even considered urinating on the fire, but couldn't position himself to do so within the confines of the cockpit! Donning his oxygen mask and tightening his harness straps, he pondered over how he was going to explain abandoning an intact fighter while holding his hand over the flare holder to restrict the airflow that was feeding the fire. To his unutterable relief the smoke disappeared, and on landing, a shaken Bob Riddle requested Sgt. Lasalle to replace the signal flag, while the charred remains of the old one were carefully disposed of. Long afterward Riddle realized that if he had only gained altitude, the fire most likely would have gone out due to a diminished oxygen supply.

Riddle learned another and more painful lesson from his habit of smoking in the cockpit, due to his use of avgas (aviation gasoline) to fill his Zippo cigarette lighter. One day he tucked his lighter into his shirt pocket after refilling it. Later, while on a mission and approaching the target, he felt a steadily increasing burning sensation on his chest. When clear of the general combat zone he loosened his clothing to extract the lighter for transfer to his flight suit. Mere discomfort turned to near torture on the return flight, and when he stripped off, Riddle found his chest and lower torso badly blistered. It appeared that the low pressure at high altitude had allowed some avgas to escape from the lighter, and it had spread onto his body.

Pilots returning to the United States usually arrived there quite quickly and without incident, unlike the 308th's Lt. Emmett Gilbert. He set off on 16 April to Algiers but there was bumped from next day's aircraft to Casablanca. Arriving at Casablanca, he hung around there for seven days before one of the other eight returning Group pilots arrived with the news that there was a ride home available on a "war-weary" B-17 slated for a War Bonds tour stateside. Nobody argued with the pilots' decision to divert south to Accra (in the British colony of Gold Coast, now the nation of Ghana) for a social call prior to crossing the Atlantic. All was smooth until the bomber was over thick jungle. Then the number-three engine started to lose power with the propeller windmilling, and the order to don parachutes was issued. Nothing immediately developed, and the men began to relax and remove their chutes, until the number two engine started to act up in a similar manner. A "Mayday" signal was flashed, and while the course was altered southwest to get away from the hostile terrain, all equipment was jettisoned. When a third engine started to falter, the decision was made to ditch off the coast, which they had now reached. The water landing was hard but successful, especially considering that the pilots had only fifteen hours of multiengine time between them! Difficulties with inflating their raft in the heavy surf, which battered the bomber into two pieces, left most of the thirteen personnel struggling in the water about a mile from shore. However, all on board managed to swim or wade ashore. Next day they were picked up by a PBY and taken to Accra from where they were flown stateside in a C-46.

By May the pilots were regarding any mission of shorter duration than three to four hours as "soft." Few sorties either had been, or were likely to be, that obliging. The bombers were ranging all over the Balkans as well as northern Italy, and the four P-51 groups were escorting them all the way. Strapped into a noisy aircraft with virtually no freedom of movement for hours, many a "fighter jockey" felt more like an arthritic cripple than a fit young man when he had switched off his engine and tried to climb out of the cockpit.

The Italian rail system took some hard knocks over the month, but in general there was opposition from enemy fighters over such targets. Ploesti, as ever, was a tougher proposition when visited on the 5th. Maj. Thorsen led the Group, and fierce combats with the Luftwaffe left the enemy nine aircraft short. Over the next two weeks, little contact was made with the Germans, even when Wiener Neustadt was bombed on the 10th.

A P-51 of the 325th FG, seen at San Severo or Mondolfo. Tail markings were black and yellow checks, and numbers denoted individual aircraft. This example bears yellow edges to its number. The 325th was one of three other Fifteenth Air Force groups to be equipped with the Mustang.

Combat fatigue took many forms, both obvious and insidious. Lt. Emery was an experienced 308th FS pilot with several kills. On the evening of 20 May, he and other pilots held a rare drinking session using the post-operational whiskey they had accumulated from previous missions. Next morning, as dawn was just breaking, Emery took off and buzzed the airfield before heading out into oblivion; neither he nor his P-51 was ever located. On the Form 1 (Aircraft Maintenance Log) he had scrawled a message of praise to his crew chief. Any pilot's loss was felt to some degree, but this was a particularly tragic and arguably needless loss. The very next day DFC awards were announced for Emery as well as for Lts. Trafton, Hughes, and Johnson; sadly, none were around to collect their medals.

The return of two NCOs to the Group on the 22nd provided a good example of individual initiative. While at Castel Volturno, Master Sgt. "Andy" Anderson and Cpl. Spellman (308th FS) had been selected for the Aviation Cadet Training program but only got as far as Casablanca, where they were informed the program was no longer accepting applicants. To make matters worse, they were then reassigned, not back to the 31st, but to the infantry! They were then shipped to a Replacement Depot at Bizerte where Spellman was appointed to the unit's orderly room. He promptly stole both men's records and they went AWOL, catching a ride on a flight from Tunis to Bari and on to Foggia. From here it was easy to

Many touring performers entertained the group while it was in Italy, and their quality varied. The reaction of the men to these gun-toting females cannot be gauged, as they are facing away from the camera, but the dancer third from the left seems to be very serious about her performance!

Sgt. Bernard Parsley bids a rather wry welcome to the snow or sleet descending upon San Severo. The resultant mud, when linked with the damp and chill of "sunny" Italy, made for horrendous working conditions in which to service aircraft.

complete the short hop to San Severo. "Andy" Anderson would later be appointed Armament Inspector for his squadron before leaving stateside for B-29 training in August.

A brawl with forty to fifty Fw 190s and Bf 109s on the 24th saw three fall to Maj. Thorsen and Lts. Day and Pensinger, but a new pilot, Lt. Knapp, was MIA. Lt. Day's celebration over his kill was even greater the following day, when he received orders rotating him home on a thirty-day leave. Over Weiner Neustadt on the 29th the Group bounced some fifty fighters and reaped a harvest of at least six; Lt. Col. Tarrant, a pilot on his second tour who had previously served with the A-36-equipped 27th FG, shared a Bf 110 with Lts. McKean and Compton. Maj. Dorris (308th FS) got a brace of Bf 109s, and Lts. Jacobs, Greene, and Goebel each downed a Bf 109. May ended with yet another sortie to Ploesti, but the nearest the Group got to combat was when the pilots prepared to engage some Bf 109s, only to take evasive action themselves when attacked by P-38s! Fortunately, no casualties were suffered, but it was not the last time such an incident would occur.

June 1944 was to prove a vital month for Allied fortunes in Europe, although the main event would occur on the shores of Normandy in northwest France. Nevertheless, the Fifteenth Air Force, by virtue of its own strategic bombing duties, not only was wearing down the German war machine but also was helping to draw off German personnel and equipment needed for the defense of the northern shores of their Festung Europa (Fortress Europe).

The majority of pilot losses over enemy territory usually resulted in their death or capture, so it was all the more pleasing for the Group to be reunited with the few who escaped either fate. On 9 June, Lt. Van Natta made his appearance. He had gone down in November 1943 but had managed to gain shelter with the local Italian citizens, who hid him in a cave north of Rome for several months. With him were two RAF officers. Despite suffering from dysentery, jaundice, and weight loss, he got back into Allied hands around the time Rome was liberated. Another returning evader was Lt. Baetjer (309th FS), who had been forced to bail out of his P-51 over Yugoslavia on 16 April after B-24 gunners crippled the fighter. His return preceded Van Natta's by eight days.

The pace of operations was being maintained, with upwards of twenty missions flown in June. Group headquarters recorded forty-four kills during the month. The Group's 300th kill was reached on the 14th, and the total stood at 333 by the month-end. Two big hauls were on the 23rd and 26th with eight and fifteen kills recorded respectively. Particularly successful was Maj. Brown (307th FS), who knocked down four on the 26th; his squadron led the way with thirteen of the fifteen. One of four 308th FS kills on the 23rd was the first registered by a dark-featured Ohioan, Lt. John Voll. This quiet man would hit the headlines in no uncertain manner in future months.

Losses inevitably occurred, and one of the saddest was that of Lt. Baetjer on the 26th; his earlier good fortune at surviving a bad crash and evading capture had availed him none. Two other losses that day were Lt. Main and Capt. Byrnes (308th FS operations officer). "Twig" Brynes had already flown with an A-36 unit and had three victories to his credit when his flight engaged a Bf 109 formation. One had already fallen to his guns, and he was hot after a second when his wingman (a freshman Lt. Col. just arrived from the United States) saw a Bf 109 curving in on Brynes and called for him to break. Brynes was last seen at low altitude in a steep dive.

Lt. John Last (309th FS) was originally with Group headquarters but had later trained and graduated to flying status and had flown a tour on bombers before rejoining the 31st. On the 24th he was with three other pilots on an Air Sea Rescue mission when Bf 109s bounced the quartet and he was shot down.

As pilots matured under combat conditions, they were elevated from wingmen to flight or squadron leaders and occasionally to group leader. Lt. Bob Goebel led a flight on seven of the June missions, during which he gained two kills. He also learned a vital lesson or two, one of which was to regularly check his oxygen equipment — especially his helmet, which was an RAF item from his Spitfire conversion course. There was a split in it where the nose fitted and which let in enough cockpit air to cause drowsiness. This occurred on one mission, when he confused another flight with his own and wound up in their ranks. A check of the mask revealed the flaw, whereupon Goebel promptly replaced it with a U.S-style mask.

Goebel's second victory came on the 23rd. A quartet of Bf 109s swooped down on the bomber formation and was in turn pounced upon by his flight. A protracted tail-chase of the rearmost Bf 109 ended in solid strikes on its right wing and coolant streaming from the engine. Closing in again, Goebel was so engrossed in firing that he almost followed the Bf 109 into the ground as the German pilot managed a successful belly landing. Another vital lesson was learned: Do not concentrate so totally on the intended target that you became a victim yourself!

This lesson was reinforced on the 27th when Goebel called out a Bf 110 to his flight leader (Lt. Col. Tarrant, recently appointed Deputy Group CO) and cut inside him to latch onto the Messerschmitt's tail. The '110's right engine was set afire, and the aircraft spiraled down. Only after return to base did Goebel learn that Lt. Goehausen had simultaneously delivered an attack on the '110, but neither had seen the other!

Around the 20th the first P-51Ds were ferried in from North Africa. This latest Mustang variant had two notable advantages over the P-51B. The "razor-back" rear fuselage had been reduced in depth behind the cockpit, and the flat, framed cockpit canopy had been replaced by a sliding "bubble" canopy which allowed the pilot better visibility as well as making it easier and safer for him to bail out in an emergency. The other vital improvement was in firepower; the four-gun armament of the B-model had been supplemented by two more .50-caliber machine guns for a total of six. The new fighters also presented a brighter aspect in their natural metal finish, because camouflage paint had been eliminated.

The first "shuttle" mission to Russia (Operation Frantic I) was launched on 21 June. It involved the Eighth Air Force, with the fighter escort coming from a mixed 4th FG/352nd FG contingent. Several of the fighters touched down at San Severo on the 27th, where they would be based for at least a week during which they would participate in at least two missions. Their Fifteenth Air Force cousins remarked caustically among themselves about the white scarves they sported and the kill marks for objects such as trucks and locomotives, objects deemed as unworthy of such recording on the 31st FG's fighters!

Effective 4 July Col. McCorkle relinquished command of the 31st FG to Lt. Col. Yancy Tarrant. McCorkle's tenure as Group CO would prove to be the longest among the Group's six commanders in World War II. He had assumed command on 13 September 1943 and had led the Group during the difficult Salerno and Anzio landings and its long tedious winter as a front-line Group as well as the transition from Spitfires to P-51s. In his farewell message he

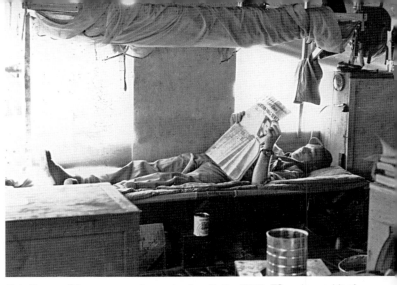

Sgt. George Gilcrease, a radio mechanic with the 309th FS, enjoys a bit of relaxation, probably while a mission is being flown. Newspaper headline reads "CONVENTION HAILS DEWEY," a reference to the 1944 Republican presidential candidate, New York Governor Thomas E. Dewey.

expressed delight about the Distinguished Unit Citation (DUC) the Group had just been awarded for the 21 April mission; he also regarded Col. Tarrant as an eminently suitable successor. The latter would need to be, because the personnel regarded Charles McCorkle as a hard act to follow.

The DUC stated that the 31st FG had flown through bad weather to provide target cover. A general recall signal had not been received by either the Group or by seven of the Bomb Groups, who were vulnerable to mass fighter assault. Maj. Thorsen led part of the forty-eight-fighter force into thirty enemy fighters homing in on the bombers, while the remaining pilots took on a similar number coming in behind. The claims of sixteen enemy aircraft destroyed, seven probables, and ten damaged against four Group losses were important; but just as important was the bombers' ability to deliver their ordnance with virtual freedom from attack and with consequent accuracy.

July also saw twenty-five missions flown with an average of forty fighters dispatched per mission. Some eighty-three enemy aircraft were shot down (the highest monthly total by far during the Group's wartime service), of which almost half would be accrued during the Group's participation in Frantic III. In turn the Group would lose six pilots.

Maj. Alvin Gillem on the wing of his P-51B *Lady Beth III*. Gillem commanded the 307th FS between 8 February and 17 May 44 and scored three victories during his combat tour. The Roman numeral "III" in the aircraft's name suggests two predecessors, which were probably disposed of through battle attrition or accident.

(Right) The 416th FS used RAF Mosquitoes for night-fighter duties during the winter of 1944-45. This Mosquito, probably at San Severo or Mondolfo, is painted in standard RAF colors of Ocean Grey and Dark Green with U.S. national markings.

(Above) A D-Day invasion-striped P-51B of the 335th FS, 4th FG, during the group's participation in Operation Frantic 1. This Mustang is fitted with a Malcolm Hood. Paint on fin identification band is well worn. A thin border of white or natural metal has been left between the national insignia and the black invasion stripes.

(Below) The slightly built Col. McCorkle has just stepped out of the cockpit of his P-51B on completion of a mission. McCorkle was a highly respected Group CO who held the post between 13 September 1943 and 4 July 1944 and amassed eleven victories during that period.

On 2 July the visiting 4th FG participated in a mission to Budapest, to which they were assigned a "freelance" role, but problems with fuel starvation reduced the Debden unit to just over squadron strength. According to 31st FG records, a subsequent battle resulted in two confirmed kills for the 4th, but two of its pilots went MIA. One (Lt. Grover Siems) barely made it back after being hit in the neck. The other was Ralph "Kid" Hofer, a top ace and the only such Eighth Air Force pilot to be killed. The 31st had better fortune, downing four without loss.

Next day the P-51s were marginally early at their rendezvous, and the bombers were marginally late. Separate attacks from ahead and behind were challenged, with two Bf 109s downed, while a bounce on four other Bf 109s cost the Germans one more. Lts. Goebel and Shelton and Capt. Wilhelm were the victors.

On 6 July, Lt. Taylor was forced to land at Ajeccio for fuel on the way back. He was barely off the ground when his engine quit, and a change of fuel tanks had no effect. With insufficient altitude to bail out or to turn back to the field, he elected to ditch in a small bay to the south. Ditching a P-51 was not highly recommended; with its large ventral air-scoop the possibility of the aircraft digging itself into and under the water was great. Taylor elected a flaps-up approach and held the aircraft's nose slightly up. The sea was calm, but the impact arrested the P-51's progress almost immediately. Barely had Taylor jettisoned the canopy, inflated his Mae West, and clambered out when the Mustang sank under the waves. Inflating his raft, Taylor was quickly spotted by some French soldiers, one of whom swam out and guided the raft to the shore.

The group's score increased by ones or twos on the intervening missions up to 18 July, with Lt. Riddle (307th FS) scoring twice. Penetration, target, and withdrawal (PTW) cover was provided to B-24s of the 55th Bomb Wing attacking oil refineries located at Oberraderbach, Germany. The B-24s did not appear on time, and on seeing B-17s under attack, the Group pitched into their tormentors. Six fell to the 308th FS, with Fl. Off. Martin getting two. The 307th was almost as successful with five, and Lt. Dustrode (309th FS) and Lt. Dorsch nailed what was the mission's twelfth kill. Lts. Edler and Walz (307th FS) and Herman (308th FS) were MIA. Edler and Herman were seen to bail out successfully, but Herman suffered the cruel fate of an unopened parachute and fell to his death.

A long wearying run to Friederichshafen on the 20th was notable for adding two more aces to the Group's total of twelve by

A 31st FG P-51 rests on its PSP dispersal surface as a mechanic handles one of its drop tanks. Gun bay doors are raised. The twin gun apertures on each wing identify the aircraft as a P-51B.

(Above) A 309th FS P-51B is raised into position in preparation for gun alignment tests, which required that 200 pounds of weight be suspended from the rear fuselage to prevent the aircraft from nosing over. (Below) As a temporary expedient, the ground crew of this aircraft has secured a 250-pound bomb to the rear fuselage as the required counterweight.

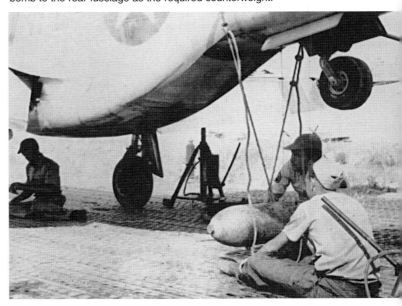

month's end. Maj. Dorris and Lt. Goebel (308th FS) were the pilots. Goebel caught an unwary Bf 109 nosing around. His initial pressure on the trigger produced nothing because the camera/gun selector switch was on "Camera Only," but a quick switchover and renewed trigger pressure sent a stream of bullets into the Bf 109, which shed chunks of metal. A half-roll to observe the stricken fighter with its obviously dead occupant gave Goebel a shock, not so much at the fate of the pilot, but more at the degree of damage inflicted on the Bf 109 itself.

Lt. Trafton had gone down on the 21 April mission, and his reappearance at San Severo on the 23rd was greeted with delight. His account of his experience was quite detailed. His number three had called in with oxygen problems and dropped to a lower altitude, whereupon he took his element down to provide cover. As he was vainly trying to get the other element to tuck in behind instead of turning into him, he sighted a large group of enemy fighters with three of them close at hand. The trio were engaged but evaded with half-rolls. At once a second trio (this time Italian Macchi C.202s in line-astern) were picked out and hit; Trafton was later granted one destroyed and two probables. A bouncing Bf 109 was deflected from its lethal intention by Capt. Rodmyre's gunfire.

As Trafton was reforming with his wingman, the latter suffered a cannon-shell strike on the cowling and jettisoned his canopy and bailed out; however the pilot chute was seen to deploy even before its owner had cleared the cockpit. Trafton vainly scanned the sky for his wingman, but the unfortunate lieutenant likely had failed to get out properly and went in with his P-51.

A second huge gaggle of fighters was coming in from the west. Trafton met them head-on, shooting down two Bf 109s, according to a fellow Group pilot (but only getting official credit for one). After a swift dive to ground level, Trafton throttled back for what he expected to be a routine return flight. Ten minutes into this final stage of the mission he was spotted by three Bf 109s that tried to box him in. A climbing left turn allowed him a snap shot at the left-hand Bf 109, which rolled and impacted the ground. Soon after, the other two disengaged.

A few minutes later came a final encounter with two more Bf 109s. This time Trafton was boxed in with the '109s taking turns making passes at his P-51 as he maintained a left-hand circle. One Bf 109 ran out of ammunition, but the other landed a solid burst in the

P-51's cockpit ripping away most of the instrument panel and badly wounding Trafton in one thigh. Pulling the canopy jettison handle brought no result, and he had to bash the rails with his elbows before it flew off. Trafton trimmed the P-51 nose down and rolled it on its back and parted company. His parachute descent was made from very low altitude, and on touching down Trafton rolled forward into a shallow pool of water, the refreshing taste of which slaked his thirst.

Concealing himself from one of the circling Bf 109s, he staggered a short distance before collapsing. A few minutes later he sighted a group of people advancing in a skirmish line. When they were close at hand, he saw on their hats the red star that confirmed their Partisan status, and he called out the few Croatian words he knew. They immediately wrapped him in his parachute and rushed him to a secret field hospital some miles distant. This was a huge piece of luck; it is likely he would have bled to death without prompt medical attention. He later recovered sufficiently to be spirited along the underground system and back into Allied hands, but the exact details were not

(Above) A P-51B, believed to be from the 308th FS, taxies out for a mission. The crew chief sits on the wing to help direct the pilot. Forward visibility from the cockpit of a P-51 while it was on the ground was restricted by its long nose. In order to see more clearly, pilots usually weaved side to side while taxiing or carried a ground crewman on the wing to assist.

(Below) This 307th FS P-51D has suffered severe battle damage to its left stabilizer. In contrast to most other aircraft bearing Group markings on their fins and rudders, the serial number of MX-I is fully visible.

revealed at the time for security reasons. His combat days, in the European Theater at least, were over, and he would go stateside within the next two weeks.

In August a new skeet range was created, and this allowed pilots to improve their ability to aim and judge deflection angles. By this stage of their combat careers, many pilots had largely mastered the art of deflection shooting — and an art it was, with no amount of gunnery theory able to compensate in its achievement. There were several factors to be considered. In the first place, the guns were located below and well to the sides of the cockpit-mounted gun sight. Correct alignment of the guns was therefore a vital factor in concentrating fire. Secondly, consideration had to be given to the effect of gravity on the bullets, which began to drop almost as soon as they left the gun barrel. The third factor related to the aerodynamic characteristics of the fighter and how well the pilot adjusted his controls. Engine torque effect caused American fighters

to yaw left, and an offset in the vertical fin was supposed to compensate for this. However, this worked only at one airspeed and power setting. Firing while the fighter was yawing would throw the bullets wide of the target. Consequently, when firing in a climb, the pilot had to push the rudder right, because the engine torque was greater than the rudder correction; the reverse procedure applied in a dive. The rudder trim aided the pilot to some extent, but its use in preventing yaw was still a matter of feel. Above all, there was the question of "leading" the target correctly (aiming ahead of the target to ensure the bullets and the enemy fighter converged). Some of the top-scoring pilots achieved many of their kills by close-in, nondeflection shooting, but what mattered in the long run was the destruction of the Luftwaffe's strength rather than the exact methods to be applied in the process.

August 1944 was a very busy month for both the Fifteenth Air Force and the 31st FG. The group was dispatched on twenty-six missions in which 1,101 individual sorties were recorded — the highest monthly total during the group's operations in World War II. Most missions were to strategic targets, with oil refineries given priority, but in the middle of the month the Allies opened up a second invasion front when forces were landed in Southern France (Operation Dragoon). Fifty-six kills were registered during the month to bring the overall total to 484.

Lts. Thompson and Zierenburg started the ball rolling on the 2nd when Avignon in France was the target; two Bf 109s — the sole opposition seen — were latched onto and downed by the 309th FS duo. The same day Capt. Molland was confirmed as the 308th's replacement CO for Maj. Dorris, who had gone stateside. "Tommy" Molland was already an ace but more importantly had a high degree of respect from the squadron personnel.

Lt. Goebel was already an ace, too, but by the month-end he would extend his overall figure to eleven. Leading Blue Flight Flying to Friederichshafen on the 3rd, his fiftieth mission, he sighted six Bf 109s, which he called in to Group Leader Capt. Molland. He was instructed to bounce them and led his flight into a diving approach. Selecting one of the Bf 109s, he hit it with a no-deflection burst that partially blew off its tail, whereupon the Bf 109 plunged into the ground along with its pilot. This would be the sole Group kill for the mission.

Confusion between the similar appearance of the Me 410 and the Mosquito caused three separate incidents on the 6th in which bogies were pursued after initially being allowed to get away. Two of these pursuits ended in the bogey evading. Lt. Busley (309th FS) chased the third and held his fire while radioing its crew for identification. Finally, as it entered a steep dive, both its wings broke off, and a large explosion tore the aircraft's fuselage apart.

The first big show of the month occurred the next day over Lake Balaton. This day, pilots were assigned to the 308th's "Outlaw" flight. (Extra flights put up by each squadron, the "outlaws" acted independently to challenge any opposition encountered en route and allowed the main Group formation to continue on to the bomber rendezvous.) The flight was flying top cover, when a large group of Bf 109s was spotted ahead and below trailing the main Group formation. A swiftly executed bounce split the numerically superior enemy force, and the twelve P-51s went to work. When the battle was over, twelve Bf 109s had been picked off. In a massive scrap with over thirty Fw 190s and Bf 109s, the other two "outlaw" elements took down a further six fighters. Lts. Riddle and Skogstad

Some aircraft, such as this 309th FS P-51D, carried a number as an alternative to an individual aircraft letter. Note the spacing between stripes on fin and stabilizer as well as the original identification band on the stabilizer partially obscured by stripes.

(the latter on his first mission) each destroyed two Bf 109s, and the squadron's Capt. Buck added a fifth. The sole 309th FS success was credited to Lt. Thompson. One pilot, Lt. Richards (307th FS), did not return to San Severo; he was last heard saying he was joining up with five other "outlaw" P-51s.

On the 10th the Group escorted bombers to Ploesti. Over the target, the 309th, flying top cover, took on twelve Bf 109s seen closing on the bombers. Four of these split downward, and the others remained to engage those P-51s that had not chased the fleeing Bf 109s. Lts. Cloutier and Dorsch knocked down a brace apiece in the resultant battle, with "damaged" claims entered by Lts. Vashina and Zierenburg. Elsewhere, the 308th turned back in response to a call for assistance and engaged several fighters, two of which bore markings of the Bulgarian Air Force; no results came from the interceptions.

Four days later (14 August) the Group flew westward to a field at Voltone, north of Rome. There the pilots were briefed regarding their part in Operation Dragoon, the invasion of southern France. They would provide top cover to the armada of C-47s bearing paratroops and towing gliders. The ensuing mission was a "milk-run," the sole difficulty being in maintaining position with the slow transports. On return to Voltone, the fast-fading daylight resulted in a scramble to get down safely. By the time the Group arrived back at Voltone, the light was almost gone, and the airfield had no runway lights. All aircraft landed intact, but two pilots compromised their good fortune by colliding as they taxied in. The next day's mission was similarly dull. However, upon their return around noon, the pilots were informed they would be returning to San Severo as soon as their aircraft were refueled, due to a bomber-escort mission having been called for the next day.

The mission to Ploesti on the 17th was generally uneventful except for the experiences of Lt. Voll and Lt. Shipp (308th FS). The former was returning to base on his own when he encountered three Bf 109s below. Using his altitude to advantage, he initiated an attack that left two Bf 109s destroyed, one of the German pilots bailing out and the other crashing with his aircraft, and the third, with coolant streaming out, claimed as a probable. Lt. Shipp was the victim of fuel pressure failure and was forced to bail out; Voll saw him land safely, shrug off his harness, and wave in acknowledgement before walking away. Voll now attracted the attention of three Bf 109s, but their prospect of an easy kill was rudely denied; Voll took them on to destroy two and probably destroy the third.

The next day (18 August) Lt. Goebel was flying as part of his squadron's outlaw flight over Ploesti. He sighted bogies in the distance but lost sight of them. As the flight turned back toward Ploesti, Goebel glanced back and was shocked to see Bf 109s closing from above. Flight leader Capt. Molland broke left on Goebel's frantic call as Goebel's element broke right. Goebel then made a swift wingover to intercept the bulk of the Bf 109s, which had latched onto Molland's element. Goebel attacked one of the '109s, and its pilot bailed out successfully. Goebel then targeted a second Bf 109; its pilot also took to the silk, and Goebel watched as the German tumbled helplessly down to impact in a field, his chute failing to deploy. Years later Goebel was to

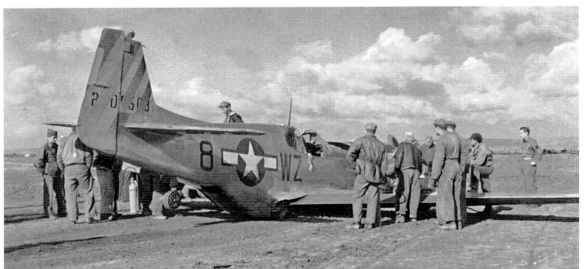

Another 309th FS P-51B with a number for individual identification has suffered main gear failure. The entire canopy has been jettisoned. Group markings on lower rudder are almost completely obscured by dirt thrown up from the airfield surface.

(Above) A newly assigned P-51B, yet to have its squadron code letters applied, undergoes landing gear retraction tests. A Spitfire Mk. VIII or IX stands in right background.

(Above) A single red band was applied to the rear fuselage of each squadron commander's P-51. This is the P-51B flown by the 308th FS CO. A B-25 is visible in background.

(Below) Lt. Bill Smith (308th FS) sits on the first of his two P-51Ds named *Weary Willie*. Center landing gear doors tended to sag while aircraft was on the ground due to gradual loss of hydraulic pressure after the engine was shut down.

(Below) A quartet of 307th FS P-51Bs shows one camouflaged and three silver-finish examples. The camouflaged Mustang still appears to be awaiting the application of Group tail markings.

(Right) Starboard side of *Weary Willie*. Aircraft went MIA with another pilot during a strafing mission to Yugoslavia on 5 January 1945.

discover the identity of the pilot. He was Feldwebel Herbert Francke of I/JG53 "Pik As." Francke had amassed four kills, had survived a Bf 109 crash in Russia, had suffered severe injuries when the He 111 in which he was a passenger was forced to crash land in the sea, and had also bailed out near Treviso in April 1944 when a P-38 shot him down. A letter from Francke on 2 August 1944 to a former Gruppe member convalescing in the hospital after being shot down revealed the generally poor state of morale within his unit: "Capt. Bauer has fallen … Uffz Zemper was shot while parachuting down … Only I, Burggraf and Kornnatz of those you know are still with the Staffel … dogfights with P-51s are deadly … we cannot get at the bombers … we have become an inexperienced mob." Francke's unhappy existence had been brought to a shocking and sudden end.

By now separated from his wingman, Goebel was startled by an impact that he took to be hits from two more Bf 109s closing at full throttle. The '109s seemed reluctant to press their attack, however, and quickly broke away in a wide line-abreast formation. They probably did not expect their opponent to pursue them, but that is what now happened. Goebel selected the left-hand '109 and closed on it but it broke left, doubtless hoping that the P-51 would find itself sandwiched between the two Bf 109s. Goebel rolled-out, as did his target. Goebel's second attempt to take on the left-hand Bf 109 was successful when its companion turned almost at right angles, leaving the P-51 free to strike at the now lone Bf 109. Goebel was almost out of ammunition by now, but in its attempts to evade Goebel, the Bf 109 flew into a slight rise in the middle of a field. Back at San Severo Sgt. Carpenter found no external damage to Goebel's P-51, but suggested that the impact Goebel had felt had most likely been caused by the engine detonating.

Adding to the 308th's score that day was Capt. Molland, who downed one Bf 109. The other squadrons had brought down five more Bf 109s. Lts. Riddle and Skogstad had one and two kills respectively, while Lts. Beeman and Busley scored one each.

Consecutive missions to Ploesti, Oswiecim (better known as Auschwitz), and Nis, Yugoslavia, followed. These were all uneventful, unlike the escort mission to Blechhammer, Germany, on 22 August, which displayed how planned procedures could go awry. The forty-eight fighters, led by Lt. Goebel, reached the bomber rendezvous point, but Goebel neither caught a sign of the B-24s nor could raise any response on the bomber standby radio frequency. The 309th FS responded to calls for help from another B-24 formation, and having driven off the enemy with the help of some P-38s already on hand (who made at least one firing pass on the 309th FS in the course of the engagement!), returned to the original rendezvous, where the originally assigned bombers, which had been delayed nearly forty minutes by strong headwinds, belatedly appeared. The now badly depleted Group and the B-24s all headed north to Blechhammer, but several fighter pilots called in to say their fuel reserves were already reaching critical proportions and they were returning to base. As target approach was being made, a mass of bogies was sighted, and the badly outnumbered P-51s prepared to engage. The bogies became Bf 109s, which approached but then shied off the attack; the reason for this soon became apparent when the relieving 52nd FG was seen approaching from the south.

The sole action resulting in kills befell a 308th FS flight that had linked up with the 52nd FG. Lts. Goebel and Tuttle shot down

(Above) The same day Weary Willie went MIA, Bill Smith survived a crash-landing in this P-51 while on a nonoperational flight. The aircraft caught fire, and Smith, who was pulled from the wreckage by two men, was lucky to survive.

(Above) Bill Smith's replacement P-51D was named Weary Willie II. It was a later model, as confirmed by the dorsal fin fairing. The white of the national insignia appears to have been overpainted with gray.

(Below) Smith's regular crew chief, Sgt. Clifford Stull, explores the intricate innards of the P-51's Merlin engine. The angled structural member extending aft from the pipe below the exhausts is the main engine support.

Bf 109s, with Tuttle and Lt. Grose (307th FS) damaging four more. Two pilots from the 309th involved in the same action were MIA. Lt. Bratton was last seen heading down after a Bf 109, and Lt. Sandler was last seen after he had half-rolled and dived after he was attacked.

The airfield at Prostejov-Kostelec, Czechoslovakia, was bombed on the 25th, and while the other two squadrons stayed with the B-24s after their bomb run, the 307th FS headed for home, having taken on several Fw 190s. On the way back, one flight bounced three Fw 190s circling Brno airfield, Lt. Brooks destroying two of them. About thirty minutes later two more flights were detached to strafe an airfield. Claims for a Bf 109 and Fw 190 destroyed were granted to Lts. Blair and Skogstad, with two "probables" and six "damaged" credits also awarded to other pilots. Lt. Skogstad was now an ace, having achieved this status in a mere eighteen days!

As the bombers cleared the target, Lts. Smith and Wilson (308th FS) attacked two Fw 190s, driving them down to ground level before shooting them down. A few minutes later Lt. Goehausen spotted a lone Fw 190, and following a long diving pursuit, ultimately shot off its tail and one wing. Lt. Voll (308th FS) closed the day's activities. He was returning early with engine problems when he ran across two Fiesler Fi 156 Storch observation aircraft, shooting one down and forcing the other to make a heavy landing.

One pilot was missing in cruel circumstances. Lt. Quigley (307th FS) had reported an overheating engine, whereupon flight leader Capt. Buck accompanied him down to a lower altitude. Quigley's engine temporarily stabilized before its temperature again shot up and coolant began streaming out. Quigley took to his parachute, but the shroud lines tangled, and he plummeted to his death in a wood.

On 28 August the bombers had been escorted to Moosbierbaum and were about to be left to the relieving P-51s when things heated up. First, three Fw 190s were shot down, two by Lt. J Smith (307th FS) and Lt. Goehausen (308th FS). Then group leader Lt. Goebel sighted bogies that turned into five Bf 109s passing diagonally ahead and underneath the P-51s from right to left. These were bounced, and three were destroyed by Maj. Lewis, Lt. Skelton, and Goebel. Goebel attacked the rearmost Bf 109; hit by machine gun

This P-51 carries on its fin the tail markings of the four main P-51 fighter groups within the Fifteenth Air Force. Clockwise from top right: solid red (332nd FG), solid yellow (52nd FG), diagonal red stripes (31st FG), and yellow and black checks (325th FG).

fire around the wing root, it fell away wreathed in smoke and spewing coolant. As he was taking on a second Bf 109, Goebel observed two Fw 190s closing rapidly. He dived away to ground level but found it difficult to shake his pursuers. He pushed his throttle "through the gate" into war emergency power and succeeded in outrunning the Fw 190s, but probably caused his crew chief to later weep at the extreme stress placed upon the Merlin engine. The third action involved the 307th FS, which ran into four very unlucky Junkers Ju 52s. Lt. Surratt downed two of the lumbering transports, and Lts. Hendel and Skogstad got the other pair. Nine kills was a cause for celebration, but the pleasure was marred by two Group losses. Lt. Jones (308th FS) was seen to follow his element leader into the attack on the Fw 190s; Lt. Wheeler was last heard saying he was heading for home.

Problems with bomber rendezvous arose again on the 29th. This time not only were the "big friends" early, but they also were 10,000 feet higher than the briefed altitude when the Group caught up with them. Climbing with drop tanks still in position placed the P-51s in great danger in the event of a surprise attack by Luftwaffe fighters, but none was forthcoming. The bomber force split into two columns, which soon became badly spread out and suffered sizeable losses from fighter attacks. Group P-51s did their best to tackle the Fw 190s and Bf 109s. Group leader Lt. Brooks downed two Bf 109s, and his 307th FS colleague Lt. Wolven added a third. Lt. Voll ended August on a high note, downing an Fw 190 on the 28th (as did his fellow squadron pilot, Lt. Martin) and swiftly dispatching two Ju 52s on the 31st.

Only two more missions were flown in August, and these added seven more enemy aircraft to the Group's victory total. On a bomber escort mission to a Czechoslovakian oil refinery and rail yard, the rear formation of B-17s was attacked by some fifteen Bf 109s, which downed several bombers before being intercepted and dispersed by the 307th; Lt. Brooks nailed two and Lt. Wolven a third. Soon after, a 308th FS flight ran across two Fw 190s and a Bf 109; the latter was fortunate to evade destruction, but the Fw 190s were shot down by Lts. Voll and Martin. Two days later Lt. Voll was again in the news. His flight was returning from escorting B-17s evacuating Allied POWs from Bucharest, Rumania, when he spotted two Ju 52s low on a reciprocal course and shot them down in clinical fashion.

The pilot of HL-H of the 308th FS demonstrates how quickly the Mustang's landing gear could be retracted on takeoff. Steel "teardrop" underwing tanks had a capacity of 110 gallons each.

The POW evacuation had actually commenced two days earlier. Among those returning were two members of the 309th FS, Lt. Lyman and Lt. Williams, both of whom had gone MIA on the same 21 April mission. Lyman related that he was about to engage a straggling Bf 109 when his P-51 started to disintegrate, and he bailed out. Taken to a hospital near Ploesti with leg and head wounds, he was amazed to be visited the following day by Rumanian King Michael and the Queen Mother. He was impressed by the knowledge of Allied aircraft displayed by the young monarch, whose stated favorite was the P-51! Remaining at the hospital for several weeks, Lyman became aware of the pro-Allied stance of its staff, which refused to act on any demands of the military authorities regarding the Allied airmen. Following his hospital stay, he was then transferred to the first of two prisoner-of-war camps, where conditions were decidedly poorer than at the hospital. Late on the evening of 23 August the Rumanian surrender was confirmed by the running about of camp guards shouting "Pace" (peace).

Lt. Williams's experience was similar to Lyman's. He had downed one Bf 109 when his aircraft was fatally hit, and he bailed out. Landing in a field, he was surrounded by civilians, who treated him politely, one young woman even giving him food and drink. He was taken to a building in Ploesti for interrogation and also spoken to by King Michael before he was transferred to the same hospital housing Lt. Lyman. His subsequent movements paralleled that of his squadron colleague.

One of the 308th FS P-51s had returned from a mission with wrinkled wing surfaces and was downgraded from combat status. Instead of being scrapped, the aircraft was modified for use on observation duties as well as a parts courier for squadron engineering and group heavy maintenance sections. The fuselage fuel tank was removed, the radio was relocated, and a second seat was installed. All guns were removed, but the gun camera was retained. A number of squadron enlisted men flew in the cramped rear seat either to gain flight-time or to proceed on leave. Observation duties entailed flying along the enemy Adriatic coast to evaluate weather conditions, antiaircraft and air activity, and to photograph ground targets prior to a mission. On one occasion, Lt. Naumann set off to photograph a Yugoslavian bridge in response to a request from Group Intelligence. The reportedly undefended site proved to be very active; the wrong bridge had been selected, and Naumann was fortunate to survive the fusillade of shells from the flak batteries.

In September 1944 the Group would account for only five enemy aircraft shot down. The mission of 2 September was a distinct change from escort duties. The Group was sent to strafe locations inside Yugoslavia, the intention being to disrupt German efforts to withdraw from that country. Locomotives, boxcars, and tank cars were prime targets. Over Yugoslavia on 2 September, Lts. Skogstad and Galiotto (307th FS) found two Ju 52s, which they promptly shot down.

The next day (3 September) the Group escorted three B-17s and a C-47 heading for Bucharest for further evacuation of U.S. ex-POWs. The same day, Gen. Twining was in attendance for the presentation of the Distinguished Unit Citation won by the Group for the 21 April mission to Ploesti during which its pilots took on and bested a superior enemy fighter force, thereby saving the bomber formation under their charge from heavy assault. The general attached the blue ribbon of the DUC to the Group's colors and also presented a Distinguished Service Cross to Maj. Brown, 307th FS CO.

(Above) A radar-equipped B-17G of the 2nd Bomb Group at Bari. The radar pod replaced the ball turret. The Group's switch from Spitfires to P-51s entailed their escorting the B-17s and B-24s of the Fifteenth Air Force.

(Below) A B-24H flares out for a landing at San Severo. Because San Severo was north of the main strategic bomber bases on Foggia Plain, it was a convenient diversionary airfield for bombers declaring an emergency due to battle damage or wounded crew members.

Flying combat aircraft was ever a potentially lethal activity, whether in combat or otherwise. A newly arrived 308th FS pilot, Lt. Lockwood, was making a local flight under the tutelage of the Squadron Operational Training Unit (OTU). He unfortunately crashed his P-51 on the 4th and was killed. A second fledgling pilot, Lt. Fitzpatrick (308th FS), was also killed on the 4th "for unknown reasons" while flying an OTU P-51.

A three-day stand-down on the 7th, 8th, and 9th was welcomed, although the heat was so intense that "sack time" was the only viable form of relaxation. Some enlisted men were observed collecting plywood, cardboard, and lumber with which to modify their tents to ward off the worst effects of the coming winter. The squadron doctors took advantage of the stand-down to check the personnel's immunization records and update them if required with the necessary vaccinations, and this did not cheer the pilots!

The 12 September mission was to Lechfeld airfield in Germany. This base was a test center for the Luftwaffe's new aircraft, and one

(Above) Lt. Col. Victor Warford climbs out of the cockpit of his P-51B after a mission. Warford headed the 309th FS from 22 May to 11 October 1944 when he went MIA. He was later reported a prisoner of war. An impressive row of eight kill markings adorns the fuselage of the Mustang.

Sharing San Severo with the 31st FG were the deHavilland Mosquitoes of the RAF's 680 Squadron, whose mission was photo reconnaissance. The unarmed Mosquitoes were routinely escorted by the 31st FG's Mustangs. Many of the pilots of 680 Squadron belonged to 60 (South African Air Force) Squadron.

(Above) The tight lips and strained faces around the table suggest that a critical technical problem is under discussion, but in fact these seven 309th FS ground crew are involved with nothing more than a poker game! Sgt. "Shorty" Powell sits at far left.

(Below) An RAF Spitfire Mk. XIV at San Severo. Later Spitfire variants, including the Mk. XIV, were re-engined with the massive Rolls-Royce Griffon and fitted with a five-bladed propeller. This variant also had an enlarged fin and rudder and retractable tail wheel. The aircraft was probably engaged on photo reconnaissance duties.

new type to pass through there was the jet-powered Messerschmitt Me 262, the revolutionary performance of which would leave the Allied escort fighters at a distinct disadvantage. The thirteenth day of September proved unlucky for an Fw 190 and Bf 109, when Lt. Skelton, who was aborting due to oxygen problems and was accompanied by Lt. Naumann, encountered the duo. Skelton downed the Fw 190, and Naumann got the Bf 109.

The P-38 Lightning and the RAF's deHavilland Mosquito had been adapted for a number of roles other than as fighters; one of these was photo reconnaissance (PR). A PR Mosquito of 60 Squadron, South African Air Force (SAAF) was escorted by the 308th FS while it photographed some ten locations in southern France on the 19th. On the squadron's return, Lt. Hargrove could not extend his landing gear and had to belly in, fortunately without injury and with minimal damage to his P-51. This same day was marked by the arrival from Russia of about thirty P-51s of the Eighth Air Force, probably belonging to the 355th FG from Steeple Morden, carrying out a Frantic mission.

By this stage of the war, ground crewmen had relatively few hazards to face compared to the pilots. The days of operating from front-line bases open to enemy assault were over. However, accidents could still occur as that which happened to Cpl. Leggett on 20 September. He was riding the wing of a P-51 to direct the pilot into his revetment, when the landing gear on that side collapsed, pitching Leggett violently off and breaking his leg.

On a happier note, Lt. Shipp, who had gone MIA on 17 August, returned from Bulgaria after that country's government had recently withdrawn their country from the Axis ranks. His POW experience, although much shorter than that of Lyman and Martin, was much harsher. When apprehended, soldiers slapped him and beat him with the butts of their rifles. The camp in which he was incarcerated was primitive and overcrowded and the food distinctly basic. His relief on being released surely exceeded that of his colleagues.

Lt. Voll was back in business three days later. Three Macchi C. 202s barred his homeward path northeast of Venice, but two were forced to flee the area after the third had been blasted out of the sky. No other enemy air activity was reported by the main escort to the B-17s bombing Brux.

A number of stage and screen personalities visited the 31st FG in Italy, including actress Madeleine Carroll, seen here arm-in-arm with Sgt. Parsley of the 309th FS.

A P-51B taxis in from the Group's inaugural mission with Mustangs, 16 April 1944. All but one aircraft returned safely, the exception being one lost to friendly fire from B-24 gunners. The single rudder stripe was the initial form of Group identification marking.

Bad weather intervened to cancel all further missions for the final six days of September and continued for the first three days of October. Flying was totally cancelled, but conditions on the ground were good enough for Col. Tarrant to order and carry out a personnel inspection, to everyone's undoubted delight! After that torment, even the uneventful mission to Munich on 4 October must have been a relief. Later that same day, part of the 308th FS was detailed to escort an F-5A (photo reconnaissance version of the P-38) to Munich.

Aerial opposition was dropping to zero again, despite attacks on prime targets such as Munich and Vienna. The 7 October mission to Vienna's Winterhafen oil refinery drew no fighter opposition at all. This was the last mission for several days, as the weather again intervened, although briefings were carried out. To keep pilots in top shape, Capt. Molland held several practice flights in the vicinity of the airfield. Less popular was the first of the close-order drills called on the 10th.

A strafing mission to Prostejov airfield in Czechoslovakia on the 11th resulted in claims for some eight enemy aircraft destroyed and twenty-three damaged, as well as forty-eight locomotives. Lt. Stan Vashina (309th FS) also shot down two Fw 190s, and Lt. Galiatto (307th FS) got another.

Lt. Col. Warford was group leader, but this was to be his last mission. As he crossed the airfield, three Fw 190s got on his tail and scored hits on his P-51 before he could get away; Warford failed to return. The flak defenses crippled Lt. Sellergren's P-51, and he subsequently crashed near Gyor, Hungary, with no parachute seen. Lt. Kiggins (also 308th FS) was seen southeast of the airfield strafing oil tanks. He was last heard calling for a homing vector, but was not seen again and was posted MIA.

Flak should have claimed a third victim in Lt. James Fisk. Passing over a hitherto undisclosed airfield, his P-51 had a large hole blown through the right wing in the gun bay. Fisk's first instinct was to climb and bail out, but the continuing flak forced him to stay low. He desperately weaved, but as he crested one rise his evasive action took him through some treetops. The sturdy P-51 kept airborne despite bent propeller tips, a bashed-in spinner, and badly gashed wing and stabilizer edges. Back over base he experienced difficulty in lowering the landing gear. Worse still,

when he started to deploy his flaps the P-51 began a snap roll. Fisk had no choice but to land with flaps up at high speed and hope the aircraft would stop along the runway length. The P-51 was able to trundle to a smooth halt.

Next day witnessed the presentation of the Group's second DUC, awarded for the shuttle mission to Russia in July, with Gen. Twining again doing the honors. Silver Stars were also awarded to Col. Tarrant, Capt. Hardemen, and Lts. Riddle and Voll.

A rich haul in locomotives and freight cars destroyed was realized on the 13th when low-level sweeps were made between Lake Balaton and Budapest. Two S.M. 79s were also added to the 308th FS score when they were intercepted by Lt. Skelton's section, both falling to him. Lt. Corp (309th FS) was the sole casualty; his P-51 was seen to go inverted and explode as he attempted a crash-landing.

A mission to Brux was always likely to stir up solid aerial opposition, as the 309th FS was to discover on 16 October. The three squadrons were assigned to rendezvous with successive groups of bombers as they cleared the target. The 309th FS found a solid undercast and no trace of the bombers when it reached the rendezvous point at around 28,000 feet. After a few minutes, Capt. Buck turned the squadron south in expectation of meeting the B-17s. What they found — in addition to the bombers' contrails — was a massive force of 100 Bf 109s using these same contrails to home in on their prey. Leaving Yellow Flight to maintain top cover, Buck took the remaining aircraft down in line abreast toward the last row of enemy fighters.

Taking on some 100 fighters with only ten P-51s on hand did not deter Capt. Buck, especially as the Bf 109s were positioning themselves for a mass assault upon the bombers. His hope was that enough of the German pilots would be shot down, or forced to take evasive action, to disrupt the enemy formation. Buck's report, gleaned from official records, reads as follows:

"I was lucky I didn't catch fire after the first one. He still had his drop-tank on and my short burst blew everything up. My canopy and fuselage were drenched in gas. Just as I started shooting at another I found a Bf 109 behind. However, I turned too tight for him and recommenced firing at the one I was after. He went down streaming coolant and smoke. (A 10- to 15-degree deflection burst was necessary to nail this fighter as he pulled right). My wingman

Two 309th FS officers gaze reflectively at the thoroughly punctured rudder of one of their P-51s. Absence of dorsal fairing on fin indicates model is either a P-51B or an early D-model, but overpainting of the aircraft serial number prevents any further identification.

reported a third Bf 109 ahead to the left who was taking no evasive action. From 150 yards a steady burst landed strikes all over him and he was knocked down. I pushed everything to the firewall and went after yet another who emerged from below. However, I got caught in his prop-wash, and when clear I found my guns jammed. [This observation contradicts a post-war account of the action, in which Buck stated that after righting his P-51 and closing for a second attack, he pressed the trigger, only for the guns to promptly run out of ammunition.] Over 100 Huns around — this was no place for me, so I left!"

In fact, Buck had much to thank his wingman for. The lieutenant calmly called out various enemy fighter positions, enabling his leader to take stock of the situation at all times.

Lt. Dorsch felt the Germans were so far off guard that the 309th was able to form up with a group of them prior to attacking. He reported:

"I gave squirts to one and slid over onto a second. Deciding to really get one, I tailed a third and blasted pieces off the cowling and wings until he flip-rolled and disintegrated on the way down. Shortly after I got a second from which the pilot jumped. Then two got on my tail but my wingman scared then off. I had real luck when my canopy fogged over as I dived after a Bf 109; my wingman told me I blindly cut in front of the enemy fighter so making a perfect target but he shot first before the Bf 109 could nail me! His team-work was perfect and gave me a chance to climb out of danger."

Lt. Swing saw a Bf 109 close on his leader and gave chase:

"He turned left after three others and the Jerry and I became separated from them. I kept on his tail until, after a few bursts on

his fuselage, he rolled over and fell a few hundred feet before bailing out. I now looked for my formation but saw only Jerries so I got out of there fast!"

"It was a real field day up there," said Lt. Beeman. "I hit a straggler hard and he went down inverted with a disintegrating engine streaming glycol. I chased another who led me a merry dance. If I hadn't fooled about with him I might have done still more damage. As I closed in after a long dive to the deck my windshield frosted over and he got away." Unknown until later was that Beeman's kill had taken the group's tally over the 500 mark.

Lt. Ernest Hackney not only scored his first kill but also pulled a buddy out of a tight spot as he followed him down onto a Bf 109. "Suddenly he veered out in front of the Bf 109 which put the enemy fighter in between. He tried to hit my leader, but my shots took effect first and he shot on down. By this point my leader had cleared the steam which had fogged his canopy and windshield, and we chased the Bf 109 into the ground where he exploded." The squadron's Lt. Roger Zierenburg scored twice to bring the final total of kills to ten — a remarkable feat in the circumstances.

Lt. Voll increased his score by three on the 17th in an unusual manner. He had aborted with a rough engine when he crossed over six Bf 109s about 5,000 feet below him. Undaunted, he pointed the nose of his Mustang down and burst through the pack of hastily scattering enemy fighters. Two of these swiftly reformed and pursued the lone American, but skillful maneuvering misled one pilot into fatally colliding with the other! Voll's score was now sixteen and fast approaching that of the 325th FG's Maj. Herschel Green, the top ace in the Mediterranean Theater. Further south, he shot a Do 217 down in flames. Lt. Skelton, leading a returning 308th FS flight, took all four P-51s down from 10,000 feet onto a Ju 88 and shot it down.

Despite the ever-deteriorating weather, the Group flew five missions in the first week of November with oil refineries at Vienna and Linz the main targets. The initial mission saw the Group give their attention to the 49th Combat Bomb Wing (CBW) after the 47th CBW's B-24s aborted. The occasional enemy fighter was seen during the first three missions, but on the 6th, just as the last bombers were turning off the bomb-run the month's first real opposition appeared. Between thirty and forty Bf 109s attempted to engage the "tail-end Charlies," but were completely diverted when the P-51s of the 308th FS led by Lt. Kennedy broke up their formation. Lts. Kennedy, Jack Smith, and Voll nailed one apiece, and Voll's flight forced one more into a vertical dive from which the pilot never recovered, all without a shot being fired! Lt. Hargrove landed strikes on one Bf 109 causing coolant and smoke to stream from its engine as it fell into dense cloud.

With the winter weather settling into a standard pattern of rain and cloud, it was the 11th before another mission was launched. There was no armistice this day in 1944 as the bombers blasted the alternate target at Linz using radar to bomb through solid cloud. Two P-51s landed at other bases with rough engines.

When the location of pilots downed in the Adriatic had been confirmed, the Air Sea Rescue services always would do their utmost to pluck the individual from the water as quickly as possible. Sometimes locating the small shape of a raft in the open sea proved too much, and the search effort would be called off. In the case of Lt. Blank, he must have felt his survival chances were dim after two nights and days adrift. When informed that the ASR service had

(Left) Capt. Jack R. Smith brings his P-51D in at zero feet for a good "buzz" of the airfield, possibly on completion of his final mission (or perhaps when the Group CO was absent!). *(Right)* Capt. Smith's fighter in disassembled form with wings and engine detached. Reason for this is unknown.

called off their search for Blank, Col. Tarrant acted on his own initiative and sent out twelve fighters. Within a mere ten minutes of their combing the reported area where Blank had abandoned his P-51, he was discovered, and a Walrus seaplane was summoned to haul him out. A slight degree of exposure was his sole injury.

Capt. Voll had a reputation for getting out of some tight situations whenever challenged by superior numbers. On the 16th he added to this reputation when aborting a Munich mission. Encountering a Ju 88, he dived onto it and shot it down after a short chase. As he peeled away he was confronted by twelve Fw 190s and Bf 109s descending on him from directly above. In the whirling dogfight that now developed, Voll latched onto and destroyed no less than two Fw 190s and a Bf 109 and probably destroyed two more before the chastened survivors withdrew. A further Bf 109 was downed by a 307th FS pilot. In stark contrast to these successes, the tail of Lt. Fuller's (308th FS) P-51 was blown completely off, and no parachute was seen coming from the stricken fighter before it impacted with the ground.

On the 19th, the Group made separate fighter sweeps over northern Italy and tactical reconnaissance sorties over Hungary. The fighter sweeps were expected to reveal many aircraft on the targeted airfields, but none were actually observed, and the night landing necessitated by the mission's duration was not anticipated with any pleasure, Capt. Watson (308th FS) diverted into Lesina, home of the 325th FG (P-51s) and 14th FG (P-38s). A strafing run over Hungary yielded fifty locomotives and many boxcars, tank cars, and trucks. Capt. Marquis (308th FS) was forced to belly in a few miles distant from the locomotive that exploded when he was directly overhead, inflicted terminal damage to his P-51. Lt. Beeman (309th FS) was also lost. On hand at the debriefing were Maj. Gen. Twining, Brig. Gen. Strother, and Col. Dayton (Fifteenth Air Force Air Inspector).

Two missions went out next day. Yet another "butt-numbing" run was made to Blechhammer, Germany, but adverse weather there forced a diversion to Trencin, Czechoslovakia. Later in the day the 308th FS supplied fighters to escort a lone F-5A on an equally long mission to Pilsen.

Strafing was dangerous enough when indulged in over flat countryside and in fair weather. The mission on 21 November to interdict German transport and personnel movements in Yugoslavia

was conducted in very poor weather conditions over mountainous terrain, but all aircraft managed to return safely.

An eight-day stand-down allowed the Group's personnel to enjoy Thanksgiving at their ease, after they had stuffed themselves silly, but the holiday spirits were dampened on the 27th when yet another 308th FS trainee pilot, Lt. Coolman, spun in during a local OTU flight and was killed. To balance this came news that Lt. Fuller, who was posted MIA on 16 November, had managed to reach Allied lines.

Although the Group was still officially standing down on the 30th, one flight of the 308th FS was sent to escort two F-5As to Munich. Lt. Shee found his artificial horizon inoperative as the formation was circling to penetrate the overcast near Ancona. When he called to say he was aborting the mission, flight leader Lt. Ritter persuaded him to remain as essential cover. The ever-worsening overcast finally persuaded the F-5As to abort, and all six aircraft turned south. On the return, they found that the hole in the overcast through which they had ascended was gone. Lt. Ritter ordered his flight to remain above the solid cloud mass while he descended to see if he could find a clearer route, believing the overcast was not too thick. This decision cost him his life. He almost certainly ran into "stuffed cumulus" in the form of high ground in the clouds, and repeated radio calls from

A P-38 burns after a failed landing at San Severo; its pilot was killed in the attempt. The aerial mast mounted above the nose and the large window on the fuselage side confirm this was an F-5 photo-reconnaissance variant of Lockheed's twin-boomed fighter.

Personnel gather around HL-G of the 308th FS, which has come to grief in a shallow ditch. The propeller blades are well bent, and the engine cowling is absent, while the left drop-tank is squashed between wing and ground. The vehicle in the center background is probably the fire truck.

his colleagues went unanswered. The other three pilots were vectored in toward San Severo by Ground Control and touched down safely.

Lt. Voll finished his combat tour in November, but his last mission was very nearly terminal. His P-51 was very badly damaged around the cockpit area by cannon shells, and the ground crew who attended the P-51 on its return was amazed at Voll's ability to keep it in the air, let alone bring it back. Voll, his face covered in blood and his clothing blood-soaked, had to be helped out of his seat, and he was unable to cease vomiting for several minutes. Prior to the mission, Sgt. John Ailsworth had seen Voll sitting on the P-51's wing in the dawn light with tears running down his face. When he approached, Voll told him he had just been informed of his brother's death in action. With such a shattering development on his mind, it is likely that he was unable to fully concentrate on the mission, leading to his suffering such a degree of aircraft damage and personal injury.

December witnessed nearly three times the number of missions (fifty-eight) compared to November, even though fewer individual sorties were flown. This was due to the fact that of this total, only fifteen were bomber escort missions, while the rest were PR aircraft escort missions requiring fewer aircraft.

Winter had now set in, and Christmas was approaching, although there was as much rain as snow descending from the low overcast. In spite of the weather, the pilots were probably glad to break their nine-day inactivity with a mission on the 2nd, even if it was a long one to Blechhammer. The month's third mission was to support Liberators, Halifaxes, and Wellingtons of 205 Group, RAF, dropping supplies to Yugoslav Partisans at Tuzla. What probably got more attention from the members of the 308th was the departure home of Maj. "Tommy" Molland and Capt. John Voll. The former had justifiably earned a fine reputation as a pilot and squadron commander. Voll had an equally deserved reputation, as he was destined to end up as the top-scoring ace in the Mediterranean Theater. That same day, Group command formally moved from Col. Tarrant to Lt. Col. William Daniel, a long-serving Group officer.

Straggling bombers were easy prey for the Luftwaffe, and even the intervention of friendly fighter escorts could not guarantee their survival. On the 11th, Lt. Hargrove was heading a 308th FS flight with the assignment to look for stragglers. A B-24 on an easterly course was seen and intercepted. Ten minutes later, three Fw109s made a slashing attack from the north, setting one of the B-24's engines on fire. A diving, turning combat now ensued, but Hargrove found his gun sight inoperative. He ordered Lt. Young, the other element leader, to take over, which Young did to good effect. Two of the gyrating Fw 190s were downed and the third claimed as "probable."

Lt. George Wilson, who had arrived on 11 November and been assigned to the 308th FS, was flying his first mission on the 16th. As the Group was in the target area, Wilson's P-51B was seen to swing erratically before falling into a spin that was still persisting when the fighter sliced through the overcast many thousands of feet lower. The novice pilot probably had fallen victim to the effects of anoxia and crashed to his death. (In 1993 a Czechoslovakian aviation research team unearthed the P-51's remnants along with personal gear belonging to the ill-fated Wilson.)

Blechhammer was another target that regularly drew opposition, and this was the case on the 17th. However, such encounters were also regularly at the Luftwaffe's expense, and this day's combat left the wrecks of eleven Fw 190s and Bf 109s scattered across the German countryside. In one melee between fifteen Bf 109s and a similar number of P-51s, Lt. Rask downed two and Lts. Cowin, Gibson, and Campbell notched up one each. The 308th answered the call for assistance from bombers over the target. Capt. J. Smith and Lt. Malone were victors here with two of the three (one Fw 190 and one Bf 109) downed by Malone, who described the action: "The first one passed under me and I got on his tail. After a few bursts he rolled over, dived and soon jettisoned the canopy to bail out. I spotted four Bf 109s just above the clouds and led my flight down on them. Three bolted into the cloud but the fourth stayed circling three or four times with me. I got him at the top of a turn and shot off his tail, right aileron, and flap." The one-way punishment being handed out was completed by the 307th; Lt. Skogstad recorded two victories for the third time in his relatively short combat career, and Lt. Weiler downed a third Fw 190.

Next day's kill total was just one. Two P-51s of the 307th FS were close to Zagreb, when a Ju 88 was noted and engaged from behind as its pilot desperately evaded in a dive. Lt. Zimmerman gained the credit for shooting it down in flames after at least two of its crew bailed out.

P-51D assigned to Capt. Jack R. Smith (308th FS) with the flaps fully extended and drop tank in place. The name *Smokey* under the exhaust stacks refers to Smith's crew chief Staff Sgt. Ross "Smokey" Stober. Name on other side of cowling was *Alabama Gal.*

The threat of the German jets, particularly the Me 262, had already been outlined in a Group briefing by a senior Fifteenth Air Force staff officer, but it was naturally impossible for the men to imagine a propeller-less aircraft, let alone one with the stated performance figures accorded Willy Messerschmitt's revolutionary design. Therefore, when not one but three of the jets swept past eight 308th FS P-51s escorting a Munich-bound F-5A, the comments over the airwaves were a mixture of obscenity and disbelief.

Any possible inferiority complex the Group pilots might have developed toward the Me 262 was scotched on the 22nd on a mission to escort a reconnaissance aircraft photographing the Munich area. The first sight of the jet by Lt. Eugene McGlauflin brought the following reaction:

"When I saw the '262 I wasn't sure what it was. I then thought it was one of my flight out of position. I called over the radio 'George, is that you?' 'Hell, no,' was the quick reply, as someone else yelled, 'It's a blow job.'

"We broke away fast and I ordered the rest of the flight, apart from Fl. Off. Roy Scales to continue the escort while we went after the jet. I had heard of the jet's speed but was surprised I could gain on him in a dive, and when he climbed I gained through tighter turns. Several times I came within 600 yards and every time he crossed I gave him a shot. On one occasion a red ball of flame appeared and then dissipated. It was his speed against our maneuverability, and we won, although he could have broken off any time."

Scales also fired at the German jet: "On his third climb he started a level turn and almost headed straight into me. He was only two to three hundred yards away so I gave a little deflection and fired. I saw what appeared to be several flashes off one wing and nacelle, and he went into a dive. At about 5,000 feet brownish smoke poured out, and the pilot leveled off before bailing out. Just as well — my oxygen system had gone out and I couldn't have followed him up again!"

The spell was broken, and the Mediterranean Theater's first jet kill had been recorded. Four days later, when Lts. Nelson and Van Winkle encountered another, they met the challenge of the enemy pilot even although his ability to close in and zoom away almost at will was clearly evident.

The third Christmas in combat saw all three squadrons flying escort for PR aircraft. The 309th FS sent out six P-51s, but Lt. McConnaghey bailed out near Cherso Island. The next day a mixed 307th FS and 309th FS flight searched the region. Lt. Cowin came under fire, which damaged his right flap; he called up to say he was aborting but required no escort. He was later reported as bailing out, and a separate four-plane flight was sent to locate him. Two smoke floats and an unidentified object were sighted near the location Cowin had reported when he bailed out.

Meanwhile, two of the five pilots engaged in looking for McConnaghey strafed some enemy positions, but Lt. Bunn's P-51 was so damaged by return fire that he too was forced to jump near Pomo Island. In contrast to the other two missing fliers, Bunn was soon picked up by a PBY. However, the day's drama was not over, because Bunn's 307th colleague Lt. Durant, who was last seen when the search had begun, had also failed to return. In attempting to save one life, two more had been lost, but such hazards had to be faced by any fighter pilot in his volatile, single-engine aircraft.

Providing cover for bombers attacking Passau rail yard on the 29th generated no opposition but cost the 309th FS one pilot; as Lt. Ryder's flight was returning to San Severo under a low overcast, his P-51 was seen in a turn at 400 feet heading for the ground. This was the second confirmed death in December, Lt. Agard (307th FS) having been killed in a training accident. In addition, the MIA list extended to six. Three 308th FS pilots — Lt. Strange (8 December), G. F. Wilson (16 December), and J. Moore (27 December) — joined McConnaghey, Cowin, and Durant in this sad category.

On a brighter note, six pilots were removed from the MIA list. Lts. Gibson, Hodkinson, and Loper rejoined the 309th FS, and Lts. Wilson and Coughlin the 307th. Loper, Wilson, and Coughlin had been absent only for between one and six days. At the other end of the escape and evasion scale, a third 307th FS pilot Fl. Off. Edler, was absent for over five months, having gone down on 18 July and only returning on 31 December.

January 1945 proved to be very quiet, with only five missions flown during the month. The nearest any pilot came to engaging the Luftwaffe occurred on the 31st. Capt. Hood (309th FS) had already aborted the mission and was heading home, when he sighted two Bf 109s low and flying toward Zagreb. He dived to intercept, but at around 6,000 feet a stream of tracer from behind rudely interrupted

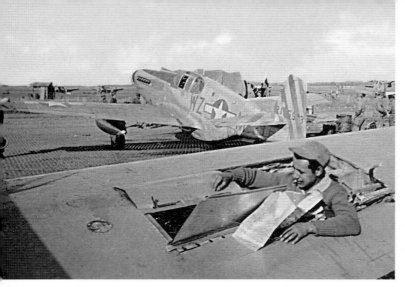

(Above) A member of the ground crew stands in a hole torn by a 20 mm shell in the right wing gun bay of Lt. Fisk's Mustang. The rear bay cover panel has been forced up at an angle. (Below) Seen from underneath the wing, the extent of damage suffered by the P-51 is even more dramatic.

(Above) Lt. Fisk (309th FS) stands in the huge hole in the wing of his Mustang. Both pilot and aircraft were very fortunate to survive this degree of damage, which could easily have resulted in the wing breaking off.

his concentration. Two more Bf 109s had bounced him from a 7 o'clock position. Hood promptly broke left in a climbing turn, whereupon his attackers also broke upwards but to the right and set course north. With his two-stage blower inoperative, Hood had no option but to avoid chasing them; in addition, he failed to spot the two low-flying Bf 109s he was originally attempting to intercept.

The Group continued to provide escort to the strategic bombers and also provided cover for a number of photo-reconnaissance Lightnings and Mosquitoes. Combat losses appear to have been restricted to one pilot, but this was not due to enemy intervention. On the 15th, as the last boxes of bombers were unloading on the target, a pilot was seen to bail out after his P-51 developed engine trouble.

A variation in escort duties occurred on the 21st. Instead of B-17s and B-24s, the Group was detailed to escort about fifty RAF Wellingtons, Liberators, and Halifaxes whose assignment was to drop supplies over northern Italy. The bombers flew in no particular formation, and seemed to drop their loads almost at random. Consequently, the P-51s were withdrawing before the entire operation had been completed.

A more usual escort mission occurred on the 31st. Two "forces" of P-51s were assigned to escort the 49th CBW and 304th CBW. The 309th FS led Red Force, accompanied by elements of the 308th, and the 307th FS led Blue Force along with additional 308th elements. The target was Moosbierbaum's oil refineries.

Lt. Bill Smith (308th FS) was making a local flight in a borrowed P-51B on the 5th when he was forced into an emergency landing. He bellied in short of the runway and had to be extricated from the burning fighter by two ground crewmen. A fellow squadron pilot, Lt. Baldwin, experienced a similar emergency on the 16th, but he was over Yugoslavia on a mission, and his course of action was to bail out into captivity. He had scarcely cleared his fighter when its engine burst into flames.

February 1945 opened with a strafing mission on the 2nd, with Kurilovic airfield in Yugoslavia as the target. One of the sacred principles when strafing defended targets of this nature was to strike quickly and to make as few runs as possible. With the 308th FS in the lead, the Group headed north. Once it was over the airfield, the fourteen P-51s of the 307th FS banked away to sweep over the nearby area around Zagreb. Kurilovic was the primary target of the other two squadrons. While the 309th FS's seventeen P-51s circled at 8,000 feet to the east, their sixteen fellow pilots approached the airfield from the northwest in line abreast formation. Their attack caught two Italian C.R.42 bi-planes on the ground, and both were set on fire. Now the 309th FS swept down to cross the airfield westward. An apparent absence of flak defenses during the first run was not realized this time around because one P-51 was fatally crippled. The enemy gunners were not using tracer, and this undoubtedly prevented many pilots from realizing they were under fire. Accordingly, the two squadrons broke into flights to again strafe from various angles. One 309th flight made an additional pass, and separate 308th FS flights made two and three additional passes. At least six more C.R.42s, a Henschel Hs 126 observation aircraft, and one unidentified aircraft were destroyed in the face of sighting problems caused by glare reflecting off the snow-covered surfaces.

The flak was becoming more and more accurate with every additional strafing run, even though one group of weapons sited on the north and northwest perimeter of the airfield was finally located and silenced. Six P-51s in all were missing, but all the pilots were

Col. William Daniel in the cockpit of his P-51D. Daniel was a long-serving Group pilot who assumed Group command from Col. Tarrant on 4 December 1944 and held this position until the following October. He added one more kill to the four shown here to finish as one of the thirty-three Group members who achieved "ace" status.

later confirmed alive; these included 308th commanding officer Maj. Wagner and 308th Lts. Hall, Lockney, Carlton, and Martin and the 309th FS's Lt. Gibson.

Lt. Hall was shot down during the third run. He eased his P-51 into a belly-landing fifteen miles southeast of Kurilovic and clambered out and watched Lt. Foster strafe the P-51 to destruction. Soon after this Hall met two Yugoslavian Partisans. Their initial reaction was suspicious; if Hall was an ally, why had his fighter been destroyed? However, he still managed to convince them he was not a German.

Three of the 308th FS losses occurred on the final pass. Lt. Lockney bailed out at 1,000 feet. Lt. Martin's cockpit filled with smoke from hits on his aircraft, so he jettisoned the canopy and jumped at around 1,400 feet. He buried his parachute and ran until he was intercepted by a second pair of Partisans. Finally, Lt. Carlton, having suffered hits in his engine, managed to get some ten miles distant before crash-landing. He sat dazed in the cockpit for a few minutes before getting out, burying his parachute, and walking away. After some time he, too, ran across two Partisans!

One by one the four downed pilots were brought together at the same safe house and subsequently delivered to the Allied Military Mission located at the Partisan headquarters at Caros. During their transit, three of them had seen Maj. Wagner receiving attention for a compound fracture of one leg; he had been shot down on the squadron's initial strafing run. There was just hearsay evidence that the sixth missing pilot, Lt. Gibson of the 309th FS, was also receiving medical attention for injuries to his leg and also a concussion. His P-51 had been seen to turn over, right itself, then crash.

Hall, Carlton, and Martin were transported by air to Bari, and Lockney followed at a later date. They expressed dissatisfaction with their escape maps, which were regarded as too small and omitted many prominent villages while including unimportant locations. There were some sharp comments about the treatment accorded them by the American personnel on the Military Mission, although their British contemporaries were highly praised! Partisan reports stated that the strafing runs had started up to twenty fires on the airfield and that the C.R.42s destroyed had been used for patrolling and harrying Resistance members.

During the month the Group continued to escort U.S. and South African Air Force (SAAF) photo-reconnaissance aircraft. On the 7th two such escort missions were flown. The first saw five 309th FS pilots escorting an SAAF Mosquito of 60 Squadron up to Salzburg. They found their fuel reserves running dangerously low as they headed south through thick cloud. All but Lt. Kratzer made it to an airfield, although only Lt. Mcginsey got back to San Severo that day. Sadly, a British unit near Pescaro reported in an American aviator's body; the dead pilot was identified as Lt. Kratzer.

The other escort mission of the 7th involved seven 307th FS P-51s accompanying another SAAF Mosquito to locations around Munich. Capt. Cook and Lts. Womack and Harper became detached from the formation after turning into a flight of two unidentified P-51s. Crossing over Leipheim airfield, they observed an Me 262 taking off. Diving from 25,000 feet, they closed up on the jet; its pilot executed a right turn, preventing Lt. Womack, who was in the lead, from getting a good shot. The Me 262 then turned back toward and over the airfield, hoping to lead his pursuers into the flak defenses, a maneuver which was repeated nine times with no success. However, the German pilot never made an aggressive move on the Mustangs during the entire encounter, and in a parting gesture, zoomed off toward Munich and soon outdistanced the P-51s.

The menace of enemy jets was ever present, as a 309th FS party, escorting an F-5 of the 32nd PRS, discovered on the 15th. Flying at 26,000 feet over the Munich area, the small group was bounced from directly behind by an Me 262, which was then fired on with no effect as it sped away. About twenty minutes later near Regensburg, an Me 262 made a second slashing attack from the same quarter. Although the escort called for the F-5 to bank right, enemy gunfire ripped away over half the Lightning's right aileron, but the pilot regained enough control to complete the mission.

Low clouds the next day caused a major upset when all but three 309th FS flights on a bomber escort mission failed to penetrate the overcast. By the time this abbreviated force reached the rendezvous the B-24s had already gone on to the target at Regensburg-Obertraubling. The 309th FS intercepted B-24s of the 55th CBW after they had reached the target but switched to their original charges from the 304th CBW when they were sighted near Lake Chiem on the way home.

Helen Miller, one of the more prominent Red Cross staff at San Severo, in the company of Sgt. Parsley of the 309th FS. The American Red Cross was well represented at San Severo by its female staff.

A P-51B of the 308th FS is caught in the act of retracting its landing gear. The center doors have fully dropped prior to complete retraction. Underwing drop tanks are of the "teardrop" pattern.

An unusual mission took place on the 21st when eight 308th FS P-51s escorted a single B-25 bomber heading into Yugoslavia to drop supplies to the Partisans at Casma; the bomber's crew safely made four drops.

Forty-five P-51s rose next day for a combined escort and strafing mission over marshalling yards in southern Germany. Due to variable and thickly banked cloud layers, the squadrons arrived at the target area separately and also at vastly different altitudes between 6,000 and 19,000 feet. The bombers were never seen despite the Group's remaining for some time. Dropping to ground level the pilots carried out strafing runs on a variety of targets with locomotives high on the list, eighteen of them being destroyed.

Once again the cost was high. Three pilots were missing and a fourth (the 307th FS's Lt. Peters) crashed fatally on return to San Severo due to flak damage. His fellow squadron pilot Fl. Off. Averett was last seen at 19,000 feet and heard to say that he thought his P-51 had sustained flak hits. Lt. Roraus (309th FS) was reported down on the deck; later on he called up to say he was on a heading of 300 degrees at 15,000 feet with his oil and coolant nearly exhausted. A second 309th FS pilot, Lt. Gravey, his fighter streaming fuel and coolant, was seen to jettison his canopy while in a 30-degree dive at around 16,000 feet but had not bailed out before disappearing into cloud.

Another escort on the 28th involved yet another encounter with the redoubtable Me 262. Six P-51s tucked themselves around a Mosquito of 60 (SAAF) Squadron and headed for Munich. Close to that city, two Me 262s were sighted at 17,000 feet some 7,000 feet below, but heading away from the Allied formation. The escort and its charge was neatly executing a 90-degree turn toward the west as the '262s completed a circle, dived about 4,000 feet, and then zoomed toward their opponents. The pair of P-51s on the Mosquito's left flank broke right, an action that was repeated by the '262s, which then promptly reversed track and dived away. The range was never closed beyond some 800 yards, and although the P-51 pilots fired in the hope of inducing tighter turns by the enemy duo, they never obliged and slid swiftly into the blanketing undercast.

What would be the Group's final transfer of many during World War II took place around 3 March when San Severo was vacated in favor of Mondolfo. The new base was located further north resulting in overall mission times being noticeably reduced. In addition the facilities were of a more permanent and improved nature than at San Severo. Although close to a beach there were two barriers to taking regular dips: the weather and land mines.

As far as aerial combat was concerned for the 31st FG, March 1945 came in like a lion and went out like a lamb. The victory-to-loss ratio was very much in the enemy's favor in the first half of the month, with five pilots MIA. Lt. Cater, a new 308th FS pilot, was forced to bail out over the Adriatic on the 12th when only a few minutes away from San Severo, and all attempts to locate him with Air Sea Rescue facilities failed. Lt. Gumbert (309th FS) was last seen while strafing a locomotive the next day. Lts. Carlton and R. R. Harris (308th FS) and Lt. Cox (309th FS) failed to return from a sweep over Austria three days later. Carlton, who had already evaded capture after going down on 2 February, was seen to walk away from his bellied-in P-51.

Up to the 18th very few enemy aircraft had even been seen, let alone engaged. Then on this date, while ten 307th FS fighters were escorting an F-5A to Augsburg, four pilots sighted two He 111s in succession near Lake Balaton, Hungary. The first was identified by the flight leader who called the other three to the attack then initiated an attack himself. The bomber's left engine trailed smoke, and it slumped away from its altitude of 3,000 feet to explode on the ground with no crew seen to escape. The second He 111 was flying northwest when the homeward-bound flight sighted and engaged it in a similar manner but making three full passes. The bomber's wheels came down, and an attempted crash-landing ended with it cartwheeling and breaking up; even so one crewmember was seen to emerge and walk away from the crumpled remains. The actual credit for the victories was granted to Lts. Scharra and Bunn.

Ruhland's oil refineries were the B-17's targets on the 22nd, and it was here that the Group encountered between fifteen and twenty-five Me 262s. The P-51s were acting as top cover when the first jets were seen coming from the northwest. These closed to make firing passes on the bombers at the rear of the formation but whenever possible avoided combat with the P-51s. The jets made a total of ten separate attacks, and although several bombers were shot down, the Me 262s were never able to completely dictate tactics.

In the middle of these protracted engagements two Me 262s were pursued by Lt. Dillard (308th FS), who closed to 300 yards on the right-hand jet as it banked gently right; Dillard's bullets set the jet's left engine aflame, and the pilot bailed out. At least five others were damaged to some degree.

The really big day for jet kills came two days later, when Col. Daniel led the Group. This time the jets came out on the wrong side of the score-sheet. Col. Daniel, and the 308th FS's Capt. K. T. Smith, Lt. Leonard, and Lt. Wilder brought down one apiece, and Lts. Keene and Erichson damaged a fifth, a credit later raised to a status of "destroyed."

Col. Daniel's victim was the last one in a group of six that made a pass at the bombers. When hit by a long-range burst, it snap-rolled and exploded. Wilder had lost Col. Daniel in the sun as they peeled off to attack, but found himself behind another of the Me 262s, and when his gunfire brought smoke pouring from the right engine, the pilot bailed out. Lt. Leonard's kill also resulted in the jet's pilot leaving his aircraft, as he reported matter-of-factly: "My shots started him smoking, and he pulled up in a slight left-hand climb. I kept shooting, and pieces flew off. Both jet units caught fire, the canopy came off, and the pilot bailed out." Capt. K. T. Smith chased an Me 262 away from the bombers, and while he was still shooting at it, its pilot also bailed out.

Next day it was the 307th FS turn to score big when escorting B-17s bombing a Prague airfield. Lt. Skogstad headed one flight patrolling the area when six Fw 190s were seen taking off from Prostejov-Kostelec airfield. As these were still at low altitude, they were taken apart by the P-51s, Skogstad downing three in the initial pass and two more falling to other pilots. The single survivor of this lethal strike desperately made a chandelle to come in behind one of the P-51s, but an extreme deflection shot from Skogstad (between 60 and 90 degrees) got the Fw 190. Elsewhere, Capt. Dillard's 308th FS flight spotted a Bf 110 coming out of the smoke-shrouded target area and heading southeast. It stood little chance as Dillard opened fire from 200 yards to land strikes on the fuselage and left engine, whereupon the Bf 110 did a violent wingover and plummeted to the ground.

The 31st FG had racked up thirteen kills in four days! Such a rate of scoring had not been achieved for some time, but there was even better to come as March ended.

The mission orders of 31 March called for each squadron to strafe in the Regensburg, Pilsen, and Prague regions. Seventeen 309th FS pilots were assigned the latter area, and they struck gold. First contact was with a loose formation of five Bf 109s, which were promptly bounced from 6,000 feet; they dropped their auxiliary tanks and scattered. As the P-51s were climbing back to altitude, they found themselves surrounded by several more flights of Bf 109s also bearing auxiliary tanks. Kralupy airfield was in the vicinity, and post-mission reports suggested the Germans might have been forming up when they were intercepted.

A series of dogfights ensued, spread over thirty minutes and ranging down to the ground. Several enemy pilots attempted to draw their opponents over Kralupy airfield in the hope of assistance from the flak gunners. Enemy reaction in the dogfights often seemed sluggish, which suggested that the Bf 109s were laboring under a full load of fuel and accordingly inhibiting the German pilots' freedom of action; at debriefing it was reported that very few auxiliary tanks were jettisoned by the German fighters. Lt. Col. Stoffel led the score-sheet with three, and Maj. Shivers claimed two (and was later granted a kill for a third Bf 109 that was initially claimed as damaged), as did Lts. Barton, Blank, Hockney, and Moore. Singles went to Maj. Johnson and Lts. Mazo, Johnson, and Wheeler.

The relative lack of fuselage damage and bent propeller blades on this 308th FS P-51D indicate that the fighter probably suffered a collapsed landing gear while moving slowly. Stains are from the engine oil breather vent; heavy stains from the vent meant that the aircraft had either been through some violent maneuvers or had suffered major engine trouble.

The 307th FS also got into the action in an unusual manner. Maj. Ramsey observed four Fw 190s strung out in a left-hand pattern as they fired their guns at a target range. The leader was pulling up and the second firing as the P-51s pounced to destroy both. The third Fw 190 had pulled up to the right, and the fourth banked left in an attempt to get on Ramsey's tail. However, he was quickly taken out from head-on by either Lt. Womack or Vernon.

And so the U.S. Army Air Forces (unknowingly) commenced what would be its final month of combat in Europe. Among its contemporaries in the Mediterranean Theater, the 31st FG was still the leading scorer, and the overall dearth of enemy aircraft challenging the Fifteenth Air Force meant the 31st was likely to remain pre-eminent.

The first few missions of the month were to escort the B-17s and B-24s carrying out their final strategic bombing assignments. Thereafter the emphasis changed to giving cover to heavy and medium bomber units as they attacked tactical targets in northern Italy and Austria in direct support of the Fifteenth Army Group offensive. A switch to armed reconnaissance missions was made between the 22nd and 27th, the aim being to interdict

During the Group's deployment at San Severo, this stylish sign was erected at the ground crew's tent area, which was located away from the actual airfield. A 6 x 6 truck trundles past the white-helmeted sentry. Hills in background were a menace to flying in bad weather

Stuck! HL-S of the 308th FS has overrun the landing strip and thoroughly embedded its right main wheel in the soft soil as well as plastering its cowling with mud.

German transport retreating from the path of the approaching 5th and 8th Armies. A total of around 106 missions would be sent out, although many of these were in squadron or section (eight aircraft) strength only.

On the 4th, during a strafing mission in the Munich vicinity, a 307th flight sighted a Do-217 circling at 200 feet. Flight leader Lt. Varous made one pass for identification, and then having confirmed it as hostile, returned to plaster the bomber's engines and cockpit. The German pilot appeared to attempt a crash-landing in a field but ground-looped the Do 217, which caught fire. Locomotives caught the brunt of the strafing, with twenty being damaged or destroyed.

The Group's penultimate aerial claim was made on the 12th. Maj. Thorsen, who was leading a 308th FS flight, ambushed an Me 262 circling to land at a grass strip. His fire from 300 yards landed on the left fuselage, but the jet easily pulled up and away, and Thorsen's claim was limited to "damaged."

Five days later, another strafing mission to the German-Austrian region was in progress. A Bf 109 fled to a hasty landing and taxied under some trees as eight P-51s led by Col. Stoffel made strafing runs; Stoffel was given credit for destroying the fighter, which burst into flames on the second pass. A Fiesler Storch was just ambling

Moving day. Several 309th FS personnel load desks and chairs into a C-47 in preparation for a Group transfer. Allied Air Force insignia appears below the aircraft serial number.

along when it was confronted head-on by four 308th FS fighters, and Lt. Hall was adjudged the victor in what was undoubtedly the Group's last aerial kill, as the light plane crashed and caught fire.

The trio of claims was sadly surpassed by the loss of four pilots in the month. First down was Lt. Aderholt (309th FS) on the 9th. He was flying a special mission to drop supplies, when just after their delivery his engine stopped for no obvious reason. He quickly turned back toward a bombed-out airfield on which he intended to crash-land, an intention strengthened by the fact that he was being shot at all the way down and would have made an easy target in his parachute harness! His wingman shot up the P-51 after Aderholt was clear. A man and woman outside their farmhouse called out to him and brought him a suit of clothes, which he slung over his arm before starting away. A young boy hailed him to say Germans were nearby, and sure enough, one immediately appeared on a bicycle. Aderholt hid as best he could in a ditch from which he was later redirected by the farmer who had given him the suit. Aderholt crawled through a field and upon emerging from it was met by another farmer. This farmer gave him a second pair of trousers (he had lost the first in his crawl through the field) and led him to a secure brick-covered shelter. From there he was escorted in relays up into the mountains to make contact with some Allied commandos — the very soldiers he had supplied! Here Aderholt remained until the 16th, when he was taken to the 442nd Infantry Division headquarters. Loaded onto a Florence-bound truck with German POWs, Aderholt actually spent the night in the same stockade and next day secured air transport back to Bari.

An armed reconnaissance along the Adriatic coast cost the 309th FS Capt. Pokorny, who was downed by flak. He was seen to walk away and managed to regain Allied lines within a week. His P-51 had taken a shell in the engine, and coolant poured out. He attempted to reach Allied lines in his damaged fighter but was forced to belly-in within a few minutes. He soon came into contact with Italian civilians who supplied him with clothing as well as directions. However, he ran into three German soldiers who called his bluff as a civilian when they discovered his revolver. He was taken in turn to Luftwaffe headquarters in Padua and then SS headquarters in Verona. No military body appeared to want to claim him, so he again moved on to Bolzano's airport and then to the town's Grappo University, which was serving as a civilian collection point. On 2 May, having again been brought to the airport, Pokarny and the others were freed by a U.S. tank column. After he was transported by truck in a roundabout fashion to Modena, Pokorny persuaded the authorities to fly him back from Bologna to Bari on 6 May.

Not so fortunate were Lts. Lockney and Harris. On the 26th Lockney's P-51 was hit by flak while strafing near Udine. He reported he was bailing out as the canopy came off, but he was not seen to jump. On an earlier mission to the Adriatic coast the P-51 of Lt. Harris was hit at 200 feet, started to smoke, then circled and crash-landed in a field. Dust-clouds thrown up by the landing prevented any sight of the pilot. Both were 308th FS personnel.

Lockney had elected to ride the P-51 down to a crash-landing that wrecked the fighter, but he only suffered a sprained shoulder. The personnel of a nearby Flak battery apprehended him right away, and the battery's doctor taped his shoulder. He was taken to a house, fed, and locked in an upstairs room. He later tried to escape by jumping out the window, but landed right in front of

Having divested himself of his parachute harness and loosened his Mae West life preserver, this 309th FS pilot relaxes while his ground crew carry out some cockpit checks following a mission in the winter of 1944-45. Collar insignia is that of a major or lieutenant colonel, so he is probably a squadron CO.

World Heavyweight Boxing Champion Joe Louis addresses Group personnel somewhere in Italy in 1943-44.

"Thanks for the Memory… ." Bob Hope strikes an unusually pugnacious pose, surrounded by troops somewhere in Italy. One of the most active USO stars of World War II, Hope visited every Theater of Operations between 1942 and 1945. He once injured a leg diving to escape a strafing attack in North Africa.

two soldiers! Reincarcerated in the room, this time he was placed under guard.

The next evening Lockney was loaded into a truck for transfer to Venice, but some thirty minutes into the journey, the truck and its escort vehicle ran into a Partisan road block. After heavy fire was exchanged, the Germans retreated back to a multistory headquarters building where they placed Lockney in a room. During the night he tore his bedclothes into strips and tied them together to make a rope, down which he climbed. However, while heading for the nearby river, he ran into a patrol, which seized him and bundled him back to the building.

A sudden RAF air strike on the area occurred on the 29th, and bombs hit the building Lockney was in; he was fortunate to survive, as one bomb demolished the stairs leading down from his room. Nothing daunted, he jumped the gap and reached the exit to end up with some Germans sheltering behind a cemetery wall. Many of the Germans had been killed; the remainder were so demoralized by the bombing and the attentions of the Partisans that they agreed to surrender to Lockney, provided he would deliver them to Allied forces. After walking for some hours they ran into another roadblock and returned the Partisans' fire. As it was by this time night, Lockney took advantage of the darkness and confusion to slip away. He was subsequently able to make contact with the Partisans.

(Above) Party of officers in front of HL-L, *Tempus Fugit*, flown by Col. Bill Daniel (front row, right). Beside him is Col. Yancy Tarrant, Group CO. Maj. "Stick" Thorsen, 308th FS CO, stands on left. Col. Daniel took over as Group CO upon Tarrant's departure.

Capt. John Voll (right) joined the 308th FS in the first half of 1944. By the time he finished his tour in December, he was the Fifteenth Air Force's top ace with twenty-one kills, a position never eclipsed by the end of World War II. On the left is Sgt. John Ailsworth, the armorer responsible for maintaining the guns of Voll's P-51.

This strikingly simple memorial at Westhampnett, England, stands in recognition of the 31st Fighter Group's unique status in the European Theater of Operations during World War II. Former original group pilot Ed Dalrymple was a member of the party attending the memorial's dedication on 6 June 1992.

On April 28th, Missions Nos. 929 and 930 entailed the support of supply drops in the Turin and Milan areas by nine 307th FS and 309th FS pilots. Takeoff was between 1300 and 1400 hours. The last P-51 of the 309th FS flight, headed by Lt. Blank, touched down at 1728, both missions having been uneventful.

Although it was unknown at the time, for the personnel of the 31st Fighter Group, the war was over. For those still on hand from the beginning, it seemed like an eternity since the first GI had stepped ashore in Scotland on 4 June 1942 to commence operations in the European Theater. Had Operation Torch not occurred so soon after their arrival in the U.K., it is possible

that the 31st would have remained an element of the Eighth Air Force ("The Mighty Eighth," as it has been dubbed in more recent times, or, more disparagingly, "The Hollywood Air Force"). Nevertheless, in their thirty months of service in the Mediterranean Theater of Operations, the officers and enlisted men of the 31st Fighter Group had served their superiors and the war effort well. They had topped the MTO's fighter group victory list with 570.5 enemy aircraft destroyed, twenty-three ahead of the next group on the list, the 82nd Fighter Group. They could now indeed "Return with Honor" to a grateful and welcoming nation.